BETTER
PUNCTUATION
IN 30 MINUTES A DAY

By

Ceil Cleveland

CAREER
PRESS

BETTER PUNCTUATION IN 30 MINUTES A DAY
EDITED BY KATE PRESTON
TYPESET BY EILEEN DOW MUNSON
Cover design by The Visual Group
Printed in the U.S.A.

To order this title, please call toll-free 1-800-CAREER-1 (NJ and Canada: 201-848-0310) to order using VISA or MasterCard, or for further information on books from Career Press.

CAREER
PRESS

The Career Press, Inc., 220 West Parkway, Unit 12
Pompton Plains, NJ 07444
www.careerpress.com

Library of Congress Cataloging-in-Publication Data

Cleveland, Ceil.
    Better punctuation in 30 minutes a day / Ceil Cleveland.
        p. cm.
    Includes bibliographical references (p.) and index.
    ISBN 1-56414-626-X (paper)
        1. English language—Punctuation—Problems, exercises, etc. I. Title:
    Better punctuation in thirty minutes a day. II. Title.

PE1450 .C56 2002
428.2—dc21

2002067551

This book is dedicated to the memory of
Miss Ida Hawkins
of Archer City (Texas) High School,
who was strict—but who saw to it that I
learned this stuff.

It is also dedicated to the memory of
Gertrude McGrath,
my mentor at Columbia University, who was
annoying—because in every disagreement
she was always right. I am indebted to these
two strong teachers who insisted that I see
the value in small things that make a big
difference to a writer.

I thank my writing students at New York University, Spring 2002, who suffered through the first draft of this book with me—their strict and annoying teacher—and made useful suggestions.

Section I: Leah Abiol, Basit Azhar, Jesse Beatus, Mahmudul Haque, Steven Kardos, Elizabeth Lee, Sang Woo Park, Pritesh Shah, Nathan Silver, Varinder Singh, Catherine Stadler, Jacob Vorreuter, Jennifer Zeng.

Section II: Amy Amargo, Bettina Andrianantoandro, Edwin Azarkian, Jennifer Barry, Deepka Chattaram, Tiffany Childs, Joanna Farah, Allison Fax, Maria Gaskill, Adhish Lal, Adam Lederman, Benjamin Milligan, Jonathan Packin, Bianca Rosa, Yana Rozinov, and Alyson Singer.

Contents

Introduction

*Thus all these tiny scratches give us breadth
and heft and depth. A world that only has
periods is a world without inflections. It is a
world without shade. It has a music without
sharps and flats. It is a martial music. It has
a jackboot rhythm...a comma can let us hear
a voice break, or a heart.*

—Pico Iyer, Writer

For more than twenty-five years, I have taught college and university students of all levels how to write. The great majority of these students can read with understanding, can think critically, and can analyze what they read. The greatest weakness I have found—and this weakness grows more pronounced each year—is the inability to punctuate sentences correctly. In my experience, students for whom English is a second language (ESL) frequently understand grammar and punctuation better than students who have listened to and spoken English since their infancy. Why is this? Because ESL students *had* to learn syntax and how the language works in order to construct sensible sentences and clearly express themselves. They could not depend on their ears or intuition to help them.

Who Cares?

These little commas, semicolons, periods, dashes, and apostrophes are small markings, certainly. However, they are essential to clear writing. We do not care about them because some self-important English professor in the sky has proclaimed them important or wants to torment frazzled students. We care about punctuation because without it people cannot communicate clearly. Clear, precise communication is the endgame of all writing.

Without the guides of proper punctuation, rightful heirs have failed to claim their inheritances because a lawyer put a comma in the wrong place in a will.

> Do you want to leave equal parts of your estate to Mary, Sally, and Tim? Or to Mary, Sally and Tim? Does this mean Sally and Tim share a portion, and Mary has a portion to herself?

Legal experts have disagreed on this. Fortunes have risen and fallen on the placement of a comma.

Without proper punctuation, a cook might spoil the soup.

> Compare these directions:
> *Add milk slowly, stirring constantly.*
> *Add milk, slowly stirring constantly.*

To assure smooth soup, choose the first.

Here's an old example that is worth repeating:

> A professor once wrote the following words on the chalkboard and asked the class to punctuate it:
> *Woman without her man is nothing.*

The men punctuated it this way:
> *Woman, without her man, is nothing.*

The women punctuated it this way:
> *Woman! Without her, man is nothing.*

Making Your Sentences Rock

> *Punctuation is the notation in the sheet music of our words, telling us where to rest, or when to raise our voices; it acknowledges that the meaning of our discourse, as of any symphonic composition, lies not in the units but in the pauses, the pacing, and the phrasing.*
>
> —Pico Iyer

Students often think that punctuation has to do with the natural rhythm of a sentence. Sometimes it does. A comma sometimes indicates where your voice falls or pauses as you read. But that's thinking about the structure of the language backward: we don't all define "natural" in the same way, let alone "rhythm." A reader doesn't know where the voice should lift, fall, pause, or accelerate until a writer gives him some clues. A writer who gives the wrong clues, or no clues at all, leaves the reader—well—clueless. The reader doesn't know when to breathe or let the voice fall, rise, or run on. After all, even a drummer in an orchestra needs a score to indicate where the beats should go.

Signal Lights

> *Punctuation...has a point: to keep law and order.*
>
> —Pico Iyer

A profession I admire, especially when I am driving on a busy street or an expressway, is that of the highway engineer. The engineer has to know exactly where to place the signs—

stop, go, wait, yield, merge—or cars will collide. It's a precise business. The same can be said of the writing business. In a short sentence (think of a country road), a period is a red light, a semicolon is an amber light, a comma is a green light. In a long, complicated sentence (think of a busy highway), these three basic punctuation signs tell you when to merge. A colon can tell you to watch for what's coming next: cars, deer, or small children. If you know how to drive and read street signs, you can transfer that knowledge to your writing.

Your Tool Kit

> *Punctuation. . .is a civic prop, a pillar that holds society upright.*
>
> —Pico Iyer

Another way to think of punctuation marks is this: They are, to the structure of the English language, what nails, screws, and bolts are to the structure of a house. Use a nail where a screw or bolt should be placed, and the structure of the house is weakened. Make too many of these mistakes, and the house will fall down. The reason for learning our language's structure is to make our sentences hold up, to make our words communicate exactly what we want them to.

Easy But Hard

Punctuation is easy, once you learn the basic rules. You'll find it helpful to memorize some of these rules, just as you memorized the alphabet and the multiplication tables. But there is a difference. The alphabet and the math tables don't change; there are no exceptions to the chronology of A B C. And 2 x 2 always equals 4. The English language has many exceptions to its conventional rules, and it continues to change. This is both good and bad for someone who is trying to learn punctuation rules: It's good because the evolving language gives you room to use your own judgment in some cases; it's bad because there are language and punctuation areas that remain unsettled, fuzzy, and confusing when you are looking for hard and fast rules.

English is very much a living language, and it continues to evolve. New words enter it every day. If you are a student or a person just now entering the work force, your grandparents were likely to have been among the first generation to use the word *computer.* Your parents were likely to have been among the first to use the term *high-tech.*

The conventions of punctuation change, too. For example, a few years from now, the term just mentioned may have jettisoned its hyphen and be written *hightech*. Punctuation tends to become more simplified as new words enter our language. You may be happy to know that writers do not use as many commas as they did even twenty years ago. And you, as a writer, have some choices, too. We tend to stick to some punctuation rules rigidly, because if we did not we would be misunderstood.

Some rules are flexible. The trick is learning which is which. The better you learn the conventional rules, the better able you will be to make smart choices when the rules fail you, or when changes in the rules come along. Always, though, keep in mind that these rules exist to help us say exactly what we want to say, and to keep people from having to read our minds. Reading with our eyes jerking back and forth across a sentence, as they try to make sense of it, is frustrating. Sentences that demand to be read more than once for clarity are likely incorrectly punctuated. As a writer, do your reader a favor: Be courteous. Say what you want to say by giving the appropriate signals (punctuation) as to how it should be read. Don't confuse your reader or waste his time.

Speaking—Plain and Simple

*Punctuation, in short, gives us the human voice
and all the meanings that lie between words.*

—Pico Iyer

Scholars who write and talk about the English language use a special jargon, words and concepts that apply to their field of study—*restricted* and *nonrestricted elements, participles, gerunds, interjections, infinitives, modifiers, conditional sentences.* Diagramming sentences—drawing the blueprint of the language and applying all the conventional concepts of its structure in a detailed way to learn how the language's parts fit together— is the traditional (and to my mind ideal) way of learning English. I have discovered, however, that most college students today have not diagrammed sentences, do not know the structure of the language, and did not learn, in high school or earlier, traditional language terms, or their special uses. Therefore, I will try to use as few of these language-speak terms as possible. Though anyone specializing in studying the English language will need and want to know these terms, my aim in this small book is to make learning how to punctuate your sentences as simple as possible. The basic thing to remember is that we want to keep our sentences from being ambiguous, or capable of being read in two ways. We do not want to be misunderstood; we want to be clear.

Know a Sentence or Go to Jail!

*The comma gets no respect. It seems just a slip
of a thing, a pedant's tick, a blip on the edge of
our consciousness, a kind of printer's smudge
almost.*

—Pico Iyer

Everyone who speaks and writes English knows what a sentence is. *All together now: A sentence is a complete thought that contains a subject and a verb: Boys run. Balls bounce. Chefs cook.*

Gardeners plant. These are your simple little farm-to-market road sentences without much traffic, and where the only sign is a red light, a period: stop. But these little country roads can merge into extremely complicated expressways that call for more complex traffic signs. As engineers have to learn to be alert, think ahead, put up more and more signs to warn drivers, writers have to learn how to give exact instructions about how to maneuver through more and more complicated sentences. For example, take this sentence:

> The boys run through the neighborhood, with their dogs frisking after them, as they chase the balls their fathers toss them, even as their mothers call them to dinner, because night is falling and it is getting chilly outside, so they must come in.

This sentence could run on forever, as more and more elements are added, but the basic part of it is still *boys run.* In the following chapters, you will find ways to deal with these running boys—even when the sentence contains eighty words or more! Learn the rules step-by-step, and you'll guide your reader as a highway engineer guides drivers, or as a carpenter builds a house that will stand up.

Commas

: — ; / • , ? ! " " ' ( ) - ;

Yet what is so often used, and so rarely recalled,
as the comma—unless it be breath itself?

—Pico Iyer, Writer

1.1 Comma Problems/Common Problems

Comma problems are common problems among student writers. Five of the most frequently made errors in college writing involve that little period with a tail—the comma.

Review comma use, and then after you have read about how this book works—that is, about Programmed Instruction—work on the comma exercises to help you diagnose your strengths and weaknesses in this area.

1.2 Compound Sentences

Simply put, a compound sentence is one sentence compounded—which, of course, means at least two sentences. (Remember: that will be *two* subjects and *two* verbs, or action words, in one complete thought.) Two or more sentences held together by *and, but, or, nor, for, so,* or *yet* form a compound sentence. Put a comma before these little words that connect the sentences. These words are called *conjunctions*, because they *conjoin* the two sentences.

Examples:

- I am going to bed now, and I plan to read this book.

- She did not eat the cookies, nor did she eat the candy.

- Paul is going to the movie, but John is not going, so I will pick Paul up.

- Did Mom come to the ball game, or did Dad come alone?

- Deborah was upset, for she wanted to go on that trip, but she got sick.

- Melissa was tired, so she left the party early, and Cathy left with her.

- It was midnight, yet it did not seem late, so we stayed out a little longer.

Trial Exercises: Compound Sentences

In the following compound sentences, underline the two complete thoughts (independent clauses that contain one subject and one verb). Then, separate them with a comma.

1. Cathy caught the heel of on of her expensive new shoes in a crack on the sidewalk and the heel of her shoe broke off.

2. Deborah thought the drink was good yet it didn't taste like lemonade.

3. Michael threw a fit for hc was upset with the dog that had eaten Cathy's shoe.

4. Did Paul go to the movie with Michael or did Michael ask John to go?

5. Melissa had forgotten to set her alarm so she was late for work.

(See key on page 32.)

1.3 Complex Sentences

These sentences contain one complete sentence and at least one fragment—or part—of a sentence. *Do not* separate these parts with a comma.

Examples:

- She did not eat the cookies or the candy that Deborah made for her.
- I am going to bed to read the book that Elizabeth wrote.
- Paul is going to the movie and may not come home until late.
- Did Mom come to the ball game along with Dad?
- Deborah was upset that she couldn't take the trip to London.
- Melissa was tired and left the party early.
- It was midnight and very dark outside my window.

Trial Exercises: Complex Sentences

Underline the complete sentence and then underline the sentence fragment. Remember that you do not separate these parts with a comma.

1. George couldn't find his son's ball or his bat.

2. Julia ate half her sandwich and left the other half on the plate.

3. I was sick of doing my homework and put it off until tomorrow.

4. The crowd booed the umpire and shouted loudly.

5. Did the men bring their tennis racquets or leave them in the car?

(See key on page 32.)

1.4 Compound-Complex Sentences

These sentences contain two or more complete thoughts (independent clauses) and at least one sentence fragment (part of a sentence).

Examples:
- I told her not to eat the cookies before dinner, and she heard me, but then ate them anyway.
- She wanted to go to bed and read the book that Elizabeth wrote, but she couldn't find the book, which had fallen under the chair.
- Paul is going to see the movie about the couple who disappeared, so he may come home late, because it lasts three hours.
- Deborah was upset that she couldn't go on the trip to London, but she did get to travel to Italy the following year and had a great time.

Trial Exercises: Compound/Complex Sentences

Underline the complete sentence and then underline the fragment. Place an *S* after the sentences and an *F* after the fragments. Punctuate the sentences.

1. Chris tried to find her puppy but it had run behind the neighbor's house and dug a hole.

2. His father told Mark that he was proud of him for having brought all his grades up last semester and Mark beamed and shook Dad's hand.

3. Robert found a part-time job with a computer company which was just around the corner from his home so it was easy for him to get to work.

4. I am planning to take the children on a picnic tomorrow unless it rains and possibly their father can go along too.

5. We took warm clothes on the field trip because it was cool outside but we didn't even have to take them out of the suitcase.

(See key on page 32.)

1.5 Introductory Elements

If a sentence does not begin with the subject (as the previous sentences do), it may open with an introductory element that tells *when, where, how,* or *why* the main action of the sentence occurs. Separate that introductory element from the main part of the sentence with a comma.

Examples:

- Discovering the book under the chair, she went to bed to read it.

- When I couldn't find the cookies, I ate the candy.
- Driving home from the party, Paul lost his way.
- Feeling frustrated, Deborah complained about not getting to take the trip.
- Bored at the party, Melissa got tired and left.
- Before Mom's cousin came from Chicago, Mom went to the ball game with Dad.

Trial Exercises: Introductory Elements

Underline each introductory element and punctuate the sentence.

1. When the weather grew warm Agnes got out her old shorts and put her sweat pants away.

2. Unless Tim comes home for dinner I think I will go to a movie.

3. After they had finished their breakfast they took the dog for a walk.

4. When I looked through the magazine I couldn't find the piece that Nick called me about.

5. Because the glass was glazed with ice the crowd inside could not see out the windows.

(See Key on page 33.)

 Tip If the introductory element is short and the sentence cannot be misread if the comma is omitted, you can omit the comma. (Example: *Finally Deborah returned from her trip.*) It would also be correct to treat it this way: *Finally, Deborah returned from her trip.*

Necessary Elements

Some elements—clauses and phrases—limit the meaning of words they refer to in a sentence. Because they are necessary to the meaning of the sentence, you should not set them off with a pair of commas. For example:

> People who have been convicted of driving drunk should lose their licenses.

Here, the clause, *who have been convicted of driving drunk,* is necessary to the meaning of the sentence. It points out exactly which people should lose their licenses. Think of it this way: *All* people who have been convicted of driving drunk should lose their licenses.

Compare to this example:

> The people involved in the accident, who have been convicted of driving drunk, should lose their licenses.

Here, the element beginning with *who* is not necessary to the meaning of the sentence; it simply adds more information about the drivers. Therefore, you should set it off with commas. Think of it this way: *Only* the people involved in this particular accident should lose their licenses. The fact that these people have been convicted of driving drunk adds weight to the statement, but it is not essential to the sentence.

When you use elements beginning with *which, who, whom, whose, when,* or *where*, decide whether the sentence would be unclear if you left that part out. If omitting that part would make the sentence unclear or change its meaning, then that part is necessary to the sense of the sentence. Do not set it off with commas.

Examples:
- My cousin, who has red hair, came late.

The color of the cousin's hair is not necessary to the sense of the sentence.

- The man who kidnapped the child went to jail.

Who kidnapped the child points out which man and is necessary.

- The horse whose saddle was loose lost the race.

Whose saddle was loose points out which horse and is necessary.

- The snow, which had fallen all night, froze this morning.

Which had fallen all night simply tells more about the snow and is not necessary.

- The ball, which had rolled under the house, was found later.

Which had rolled under the house simply tells more about the ball and is not necessary.

Notice the differences between these three sentences:
- The train running through Virginia headed South.

All words are necessary words.

- The train, which runs through Virginia, headed South.

It may be helpful to know that this train runs through Virginia, but the sentence basically means to convey that the train is headed South. Therefore the *which* phrase is unnecessary.

• The train that runs through Virginia headed South.

Here, the train that runs through Virginia—as opposed to the train that runs through another state—headed South. These are necessary words.

 Tip The words *that* and *which* are often used interchangeably in a sentence. *That* introduces a part that is almost always necessary in the sentence, and *which* introduces a part that is often not necessary. (*That* often points out a specific subject, and *which* often adds more information about a subject.) A good general rule is to place a comma before *which*, but do not place a comma before *that*.

Examples:

• The car that was brand new when I bought it has broken down.

The *that* phrase is a necessary of the sentence; it points out the specific car—the one that was brand new.

However

• The car, which was brand new when I bought it, has broken down.

The *which* phrase simply tells more about the car that has broken down. The basic sentence is: The car has broken down. So the *which* phrase is not necessary to the sense of the sentence. Therefore, it should be set off with commas.

Appositives

The word "appositive" means a "renaming" of a noun or a pronoun that has already been named. For example: Michael, my very best friend, lied to me. (*My very best friend* is an appositive, which renames Michael, and should be set off with commas.)

Examples:

- *Pride and Prejudice,* a book by Jane Austen, is my favorite novel.
- Houston, the largest city in Texas, was named for Sam Houston.

Trial Exercises: Necessary Elements

Draw a line under the *unnecessary* words introduced by *which*, *who*, *whom*, *when*, or *where* in the sentences below.

1. The speaker who had risen from his chair to begin his talk fell off the dais.

2. The athletes for whom the party was given broke into singing the school song.

3. The dog that ran under the chair was the one who had eaten her shoe.

4. The truck that chugged around the corner finally broke down across the street.

(See key on page 33.)

Trial Exercises: More Necessary Elements

Try another set. Underline the *unnecessary* element in each sentence.

1. The clock which had been ticking very loudly burst a spring and flew off the wall.

2. Down in the valley where the grass is grecner than it is anywhere else you can see the men at work on tractors and other equipment.

3. My friends Hannah and Rebecca whom I haven't seen for six years are coming to visit me this week.

4. The old car that sat in the driveway all winter was finally hauled away.

5. The man who broke into our house while we were away was arrested.

(See key on page 34.)

1.6 Parenthetical Comments

Related to necessary and unnecessary elements in a sentence are parenthetical comments. These are comments that can be left out—little asides the writer throws in to add color, or personality, or to give his writing a special style. We call these "parenthetical comments" because they could very well be put in parentheses in the sentence, but parentheses can sometimes clutter up your writing style, keeping it from flowing gracefully. Sometimes you may want to use them; sometimes you may want to use a pair of commas instead because they are less intrusive.

Example:

> Melissa carried her gloves everywhere she went (in her pocket, in her handbag) because she thought they brought her good luck.

The words in parentheses are not necessary to the meaning of the sentence, but they add color and personality to the writing style. In this example, parentheses work quite well because the parenthetical comment follows a complete thought, and that unnecessary element calls for a comma itself. Adding another could clutter the sentence. In the following sentence, however, commas work better to offset the parenthetical comment.

"Oh, I forgot, Deborah wants you to call her."

"Oh, I forgot," is a parenthetical comment. The main thing the writer wants to say is that *Deborah wants you to call her.* It would look awkward at the beginning of a sentence to use parentheses, so it is more graceful to set these words off in a pair of commas instead.

Trial Exercises: Parenthetical Elements
Underline the parenthetical elements in these sentences; then punctuate the sentences.

1. Believe it or not I haven't been home a single night this week.

2. I know Susan was at the party I spoke with her myself but she may have left early.

3. Then I thought oh dear I've lost my wallet.

4. I have an idea let's call Robert and Jill and take them out for dinner.

5. Your mother called and oh yes she said you left your history book at home.

(See key on page 34.)

1.7 Items in a Series
When you use three or more words in a series, put a comma after each word in the series. (I know, I know, your last teacher told you to put a comma after all words in a series except the last. But we're making this simple, right? You will never be wrong if you put a comma after every word in a series, and you

might sometimes be wrong if you left the final comma out. So do it this way, okay?)

Examples:

- The vendor sells hot dogs, pretzels, hamburgers, and soft drinks.

- For my birthday I got a sweater, a pair of gloves, a hat, and several other items.

- It makes me wild, mad, crazy, and frustrated when teachers give contradictory instructions on where to place commas!

Trial Exercises: Items in a Series

Let's do something easy. Place commas where they are needed in these sentences.

This is a no-brainer. When you're finished, go back and do all the punctuation exercises again. Do them over and over until they become a part of you.

1. Your brother dropped by with your suitcase blanket lamp books and box of junk.

2. The corn beans squash tomatoes and various things I don't recognize are coming up the garden.

3. If you're going upstairs please carry this basket of clothes that pile of mail and whatever those things are over there in the corner.

4. She'd tried her hair long she'd tried her hair short and this time she thought she might try a buzz cut.

5. He collected stamps from Great Britain Ireland Spain France Italy Switzerland and Germany.

(See key on page 35.)

1.8 Key to Trial Exercises

Compound Sentences

1. Cathy caught the heel of one of her expensive new shoes in a crack on the sidewalk, and the heel of her shoe broke off.

2. Deborah thought the drink was good, yet it didn't taste like lemonade.

3. Michael threw a fit, for he was upset with the dog that had eaten Cathy's shoe.

4. Did Paul go to the movie with Michael, or did Michael ask John to go?

5. Melissa had forgotten to set her alarm, so she was late for work.

Complex Sentences

1. George couldn't find his son's ball or his bat.

2. Julia ate half her sandwich and left the other half on the plate.

3. I was sick of doing my homework and put it off until tomorrow.

4. The crowd booed the umpire and shouted loudly.

5. Did the men bring their tennis racquets or leave them in the car?

Compound/Complex Sentences

1. Chris tried to find her puppy, (S) but it had run behind the neighbor's house (S) and dug a hole. (F)

2. His father told Mark that he was proud of him for having brought all his grades up last semester, (S) and Mark beamed, (S) and shook Dad's hand. (F)

3. Robert found a part-time job with a computer company,

(S) which was just around the corner from his home, (F) so it was easy for him to get to work. (S)

4. I am planning to take the children on a picnic tomorrow, (S) unless it rains, (F) and possibly their father can go along too. (S)

5. We took warm clothes on the field trip, (S) because it was cool outside, (F) but we didn't even have to take them out of the suitcase. (S)

Introductory Elements

1. When the weather grew warm, Agnes got out her old shorts and put her sweat pants away.

2. Unless Tim comes home for dinner, I think I will go to a movie.

3. After they had finished their breakfast, they took the dog for a walk.

4. When I looked through the magazine, I couldn't find the piece that Nick called me about.

5. Because the glass was glazed with ice, the crowd inside could not see out the window.

Necessary Elements

1. The speaker, who had risen from his chair to begin his talk, fell off the dais.

2. The athletes, for whom the party was given, broke into singing the school song.

3. The dog that ran under the chair was the one who had eaten her shoe.
   All parts are necessary. Remember the rule of *that*.

4. The truck that chugged around the corner finally broke down across the street.
   All parts are necessary.

More Necessary Elements

1. The clock, which had been ticking very loudly, burst a spring and flew off the wall.

2. Down in the valley, where the grass is greener than it is anywhere else, you can see the men at work on tractors and other equipment.

3. My friends, Hannah and Rebecca, are coming to visit me this week. (*Hannah and Rebecca* are appositives. Place commas around them.)

4. The old car that sat in the driveway all winter was finally hauled away.

    All parts are necessary.

5. The man who broke into our house while we were away was arrested.

    All parts are necessary.

Parenthetical Elements

1. Believe it or not, I haven't been home a single night this week.

2. I know Susan was at the party, I spoke with her myself, but she may have left early.

3. Then I thought, oh dear, I've lost my wallet.

4. I have an idea, let's call Robert and Jill and take them out for dinner.

5. Your mother called and, oh yes, she said you left your history book at home.

Items in a Series

1. Your brother dropped by with your suitcase, blanket, lamp, books, and box of junk.

2. The corn, beans, squash, tomatoes, and various things I don't recognize are coming up in the garden.

3. If you're going upstairs, please carry this basket of clothes, that pile of mail, and whatever those things are over there in the corner.

4. She'd tried her hair long, she'd tried her hair short, and this time she thought she might try a buzz cut.

5. He collected stamps from Great Britain, Ireland, Spain, France, Italy, Switzerland, and Germany.

1.9 Programmed Instruction

A programmed text teaches by leading students through their own learning without the help of a teacher. You will strengthen your skills as you go along, building on each skill you have acquired. This kind of instruction allows you to review what you have learned, practice a skill again and again, and develop confidence in your ability to use punctuation to express yourself clearly and precisely. (Remember, though, you will have my voice in your ear as you work on these exercises.)

1.10 Diagnostic Exercises

Below are some exercises based on the comma rules above. Do the exercises and test yourself. Then check your answers on page 38, where you will find some further tips to help you remember these comma rules.

Punctuate the following sentences.

1. Throughout these four essays a theme of fitting into society is found.

2. Jim had forgotten to change his watch to daylight saving time so he missed the first meeting of the day.

3. In the essay "Ring Leader" the writer does not try to hide her peculiarities but becomes more forceful in making them apparent.

4. He was speaking to me his sister as if I were a child.

5. Nick told me that Natalie was an employee of the college the wife of a professor.

6. When I looked the car over I saw that its tire seemed to be losing air so I drove to the station on the corner and filled it up.

7. From start to finish the defense insisted that the one and only issue in the case was whether the college had deprived Jane of her right to free speech.

8. The teacher thought of Janet the single mother in one of her classes who cooked in a diner all day and came to school at night worn out.

9. She filed an official grievance which worked its way through the institutional process.

10. Even though Matt was angry with Carrie he decided to call her anyway.

11. I realized that I could gain another 15 minutes of sleep if I went to class in my pajamas but I noticed that my fellow classmates had made the same discovery.

12. From changing our hairstyles to changing our physical appearances surgically some of us have strong desires to conform to society's demands to fit in.

13. Society is no help for it tells us again and again that we can most be ourselves by looking like someone else.

14. From the moment I got out of bed and answered the phone today great things began to happen.

15. She was not in the popular group and she wished that she could feel accepted by her peers.

16. The paper which she finally decided to write on an aspect of the Civil War received an A.

17. The newspaper that covered the story misspelled my name.

18. My aunt Mary Ann said that her inn was filled over the Thanksgiving holiday.

19. When we bought the new house Josie helped paint all the downstairs rooms.

20. For the reunion my family came from England France Italy and South Dakota.

21. While the children sang in the recital their parents watched with rapt attention.

22. She cared so much about the way others looked at her that she forgot what really matters which is feeling comfortable with oneself.

23. He rooted for his home baseball team and he wished it would win more often.

24. As she grew older Anna found that her home and garden became more important to her.

25. Leah and her suitemates Carla Heather Jessica and Samantha went skiing during winter break.

1.11 Key to Diagnostic Exercises

1. Throughout these four essays, a theme of fitting into society is found.

   The first four words are an introductory element and should be followed by a comma.

2. Jim had forgotten to change his watch to daylight saving time, so he missed the first meeting of the day.

   This is a compound sentence connected by the conjunction *so*.

3. In the essay, "Ring Leader," the narrator does not try to hide her peculiarities but becomes more forceful in making them apparent.

   Here, *essay* and "Ring Leader" refer to the same subject. "Ring Leader" simply renames "essay." This appositive is set off in commas. Notice that the comma is placed *inside* the quotation mark. Remember that commas always go inside quotation marks. Also notice that there is no comma before *but*. Why? Because the words that *but* introduces here are not a complete sentence. This sentence contains one complete sentence and one sentence fragment; therefore, it is a *complex sentence*.

4. He was speaking to me, his sister, as if I were a child.

   Me and *his sister* are the same person; therefore, this appositive is set off with commas.

5. Nick told me that Natalie was an employee of the college, the wife of a professor.

   Again we have an appositive: *wife of a professor* renames *Natalie*.

6. When I looked the car over, I saw that its tire seemed to be losing air, so I drove to the station on the corner and filled it up.

   The six-word introductory element is followed by a comma. This is followed by two complete thoughts—a compound construction—joined together by the conjunction *so*. A comma is placed before the conjunction.

7. From start to finish, the defense insisted that the one and only issue in the case was whether the college had deprived Jane of her right to free speech.

   This sentence begins with an introductory element, which is followed by a comma. If the comma were omitted, you would still not be likely to misread the sentence. Therefore, the comma here is optional. The rest of the sentence needs no punctuation.

8. The teacher thought of Janet, the single mother in one of her classes who cooked in a diner all day and came to school at night worn out.

   Janet and *the single mother who cooked and came to school* refer to the same person. The rest of the sentence after *Janet* simply renames Janet. You might be tempted to place a comma before *who* and after *day,* but this would be a mistake.

9. She filed an official grievance, which worked its way through the institutional process.

   Remember the comma before *which.*

10. Even though Matt was angry with Carrie, he decided to call her anyway.

    The introductory element is followed by a comma. You might see this as an optional comma, since the sentence is unlikely to be misread without it.

11. I realized that I could gain another fifteen minutes of sleep if I went to class in my pajamas, but I noticed that my fellow classmates had made the same discovery.

This is a compound sentence—two complete thoughts joined by *but,* so you need a comma. If you left out the *I* after *but,* you would have a complex sentence that would not require a comma.

12. From changing our hairstyles to changing our physical appearances surgically, some of us have strong desires to conform to society's demands to fit in.

The comma follows an introductory element.

13. Society is no help, for it tells us again and again that we can most be ourselves by looking like someone else.

A compound sentence with its two complete thoughts joined by *for* requires a comma.

14. From the moment I got out of bed and answered the phone today, great things began to happen.

Notice that the introductory element here is longer than the basic part of the sentence that follows it. This kind of construction, punctuated properly with a comma, often lends emphasis to the final words in the sentence.

15. She was not in the popular group, and she wished that she could feel accepted by her peers.

Follow the compound sentence rule here—two complete thoughts joined by *and*. Remember that if the sentence read like this, "She was not in the popular group and wished that she could feel accepted by her peers," it would operate under the complex sentence rule and would not require a comma.

16. The paper, which she finally decided to write on an aspect of the Civil War, received an A.

Remember the comma before *which*. The major part of the sentence is this: The paper received an A. All the other words are not necessary to the sense of the sentence, though they may enrich it.

17. The newspaper that covered the story misspelled my name.

No punctuation needed. Remember that you usually do not need a comma before *that* because in most cases it introduces words necessary to the sentence. We are not speaking about any old newspaper here; rather, we are speaking about the newspaper that covered the story.

18. My aunt, Mary Ann, said that her inn was filled over the Thanksgiving holiday.

Mary Ann renames *aunt*—an appositive—and requires a comma. If the sentence read, "My Aunt Mary Ann..." *Aunt* would become a title, rather than an appositive and would not call for a comma. Think of Grandma Moses, Uncle Sam. In the unlikely case that you wrote, "My grandma, Moses," you would be renaming grandma, not using the word as a title.

19. When he bought the new house, Josie helped paint all the downstairs rooms.

Use a comma after an introductory element.

20. For the reunion, my family came from England, France, Italy, and South Dakota.

The first three words are an introductory element and require a comma. The other commas punctuate words in a series—and remember the final comma before *and*.

21. When the children sang in the recital, their parents watched with rapt attention.

Again, this is a sentence that opens with an introductory element, which requires a comma.

[41]

22. She cared so much about the way others looked at her that she forgot what really matters, which is feeling comfortable with oneself.

The unnecessary words here are preceded by a comma. Notice that *that* is essential to the sentence, so it is not preceded by a comma.

23. He rooted for his home baseball team, and he wished it would win more often.

A compound sentence calls for a comma to separate its two complete thoughts. Remember: If there were no subject, *he,* in the part of the sentence after the comma, you would not need that comma. The sentence would then be complex.

24. As she grew older, Anna found that her home and garden became more important to her.

Use a comma after an introductory element.

25. Leah and her suitemates, Carla, Heather, Jessica, and Samantha, went skiing during winter break.

Notice that Carla, Heather, Jessica, and Samantha not only fall under the *words in a series rule,* but they are also appositives of *suitemates.* Therefore, you must place a comma after *Samantha* here, too, since that name closes the appositive.

1.12 Review: Your Toolbox

You can't depend on your ear to guide you when punctuating your sentences. And you can't punctuate correctly by anticipating where you think you may want to breathe or let your voice fall when reading. *You can't write with rhythm until you learn the drummer's music score; the engineer's road signs: stop (period), go (comma), merge (semicolon), watch for deer (colon);*

or the builder's tools: that box of nuts and bolts and nails and screws that keep a structure standing up.

Commas (and that simple little period) are the gear in your bag that will go a long way toward making you a good writer, that is, a writer who doesn't confuse his reader.

- Use commas before words that join compound sentences.

- Don't use commas to join a sentence and a fragment or to join two sentences with no conjunction.

- Place commas after introductory elements within a sentence.

- Use commas in pairs to set off parenthetical elements in a sentence.

- Use commas when listing three or more items in a series.

Punctuate this sentence:

I will never again forget to use a comma before a conjunction in compound sentences and I will forgo using commas to join a sentence and a sentence fragment or to join two sentences without a conjunction and by no means will I forget to use a comma after an introductory element in a sentence while I will of course remember to use pairs of commas to set off unnecessary and parenthetical elements and just to prove I am a master at using the almighty comma I will forever use one after every single item when I list words in a series such as period comma and semicolon. Amen.

Writer's Pledge

I will never again forget to use a comma before a conjunction in compound sentences, and I will forgo using commas to join a sentence and a sentence fragment, or to join two sentences without a conjunction, and by no means will I forget to use a comma after an introductory element in a sentence, while I will, of course, remember to use pairs of commas to set off unnecessary and parenthetical elements, and just to prove I am a master at using the almighty comma, I will forever use one after every single item, when I list words in a series, such as period, comma, and semicolon. Amen.

End Punctuation

2

No iron can pierce the heart with such force as a period put at just the right place.

—Isaac Babel, Author

Perhaps by now you wish this book would do exactly what this chapter title indicates: end punctuation—forever. No such luck. We are now about to answer the question: What do writers put at the ends of sentences. This part is fairly simple, compared to exactly how a writer uses commas. But you have to stay alert.

2.1 Periods

Everyone knows we put periods after sentences that make statements, give mild commands, or make mild requests.

Examples:
- I will not go to another sale at the department store.
- You should never go to a sale at the department store.

- Please do not slam the door when you go to the sale at the department store.

▶ **Periods should also be placed at the ends of sentences that close indirect questions.**

Indirect questions simply report what one asks, rather than actually ask a question.

Examples:

- I asked him how many times this year he had been to a sale at that department store.

- We're all wondering when the sale at the department store will begin.

▶ **We also put periods after sentence fragments that are used for stylistic effect.**

Example:

I'm going shopping. But not at that department store.

▶ **We use a period after an abbreviation.**

Examples:

Dr.	Jr.	Ms.
G.B.	M.A.	Ph.D.
Gen.	Mr.	Prof.
J.D.	Mrs.	U.S.A.

Use periods after a.m. and p.m., because these are abbreviations for *ante meridian* and *post meridian*. When you write company names in abbreviation, use periods after them:

| Inc. | Co. | Corp. |

But these should be used only when you are abbreviating official names; otherwise, write them out: incorporated, company, corporation.

Example:

> I do business with Citibank Corp.
>
> The corporation I do my banking with is Citibank.

The common abbreviation, *etc.* (*etcetera* meaning "and so forth") calls for a period.

> She filed legal documents, correspondences,
> contracts, *etc.*

When you write academic papers at a university, you will often be asked to use special abbreviations in citations, such as *e.g.* (for example), *et al.* (and others), *i.e.* (that is). Each profession has its special abbreviations, so when you are writing about, or writing to, someone in a particular profession, you should seek out an appropriate directory for that profession.

 Tip) If your sentence ends with an abbreviation having a period after it, don't add a final period. One period is sufficient.

Examples:

- He was a new immigrant to the U.S.
- He signs his name Barney Rubble, J.D.
- His signature reads Barney Fife, M.D.
- He is now Barney Miller, Ph.D., Hon.

Some abbreviations have no periods at all.

Examples:

FBI	DDT	AM
CIA	UNESCO	FM

▶ **If you write a quotation within a sentence, use only one period at the end of the sentence.**

Examples:

- Mom said, "I don't want you to go out in this nasty weather," but I wanted to go skiing.

- When I was outside raking leaves, Dad made me an offer I couldn't refuse—"I'll give you fifty dollars to clean the garage," he said—so I did it.

2.2 Question Marks

Punctuation, in short, gives us the human voice, and all the meanings that lie between the words. 'You aren't young, are you?' loses its innocence when it loses the question mark."

—Pico Iyer

▶ **A question mark, of course, comes at the end of a question.**

Examples:

- What do you want to do tonight?

- I don't know, Marty, what do you want to do?

▶ **It is also used to indicate surprise or skepticism.**

Examples:

- What? He can't come? Doesn't he know I already have the tickets?

- So? What did you think would happen?

When you write a sentence that contains a series of questions, you have a couple of choices.

What do you want on your pizza? Double cheese? Veggies? Sausage? Pepperoni?

Or you can write:

> What do you want on your pizza—double cheese, veggies, sausage, pepperoni?

When you write a question within a quotation, use a comma at the end of the sentence, and start the question with a capital letter.

> He had asked her repeatedly, "What do you want on your pizza?"

When the introductory element is an independent clause directing attention to a quote, use a colon.

> It made her crazy, because she thought he would never stop asking the question: "What do you want on your pizza?"

When you want to add a comment after the question, continue your sentence without capitalizing the word after the question mark—in this case *so*.

> It made her crazy, because she thought he would never stop asking the question: "What do you want on your pizza? What do you want on your pizza?" so she shook her head and said, "I'd just rather have a hamburger."

When a sentence ends with a question mark, do not add a final period. One punctuation mark will suffice.

> Pizza, pizza, pizza. Is that all you can talk about?

2.3 Exclamation Points

> *Add an exclamation point to 'To be or not to be…' and the gloomy Dane has all the resolve he needs…*
>
> —Pico Iyer

If a period at the end of a sentence is a red light telling the reader to stop, an exclamation point is the horn on your car telling the reader to look out. Don't use that blasting horn often. Use exclamation marks sparingly. If you succeed in building the excitement into your sentences, you won't need an exclamation point to tell the reader how to read them.

Example:

> I was running down the dark alley when my shoe heel caught in the grate, so I fell down on my knees, and when I looked up a person in a ski mask had a gun in my face.

You don't need an exclamation point here. The fear in the voice of the person speaking creates the reader's excitement.

But you may want to use exclamation points in a quotation or when writing dialogue.

Examples:

- She said, "I was running down the dark alley when my shoe heel caught in the grate, so I fell down on my knees, and when I looked up a person in a ski mask had a gun in my face!"

- "He has a gun!" I yelled.

- "Get out of his way!"

- "Did he get your wallet?"

Though the person speaking may very well be excited, do not use an exclamation point after the question mark. One punctuation mark is sufficient.

2.4 Exercises

Punctuate the sentences below.

1. I wanted to go for a hike and a swim but Deborah was visiting and wouldn't leave

2. "Do you want to go for a hike and a swim with Cathy and me" I asked her

3. "How long do you think you'll be gone" she asked

4. We told her we'd be gone for about three hours but wanted to know when she had to be back

5. "Oh about four p m " she said "Is that okay "

6. "Why that soon" Cathy asked

7. "I have to call Mr Shaw about the plumbing in my dorm and write a letter to Prof Crosby about my paper that is due next week for my 9 a m class "

8. I asked her if there was a problem with her paper

9. "No" she replied "but Prof Crosby Prof Johnson and Prof Conner etc all assigned the same due date for their papers Can you believe that Don't they ever talk to one another"

10. I wondered whether Deborah would have a hard time getting all the papers in on the same day

11. "Maybe you could ask Prof Crosby for an extension He's pretty reasonable isn't he "

12. "I was thinking of that" she said "Do you think he would mind "

13. Cathy wasn't listening so she asked "Who are you talking about "

14. Deborah told her never mind then asked when we were leaving for a hike

15. "What time do you want to leave " I asked her

16. "Right now" she said then asked whether we could stop and pick up her books her jeans and her jogging shoes on the way

17. Cathy didn't hear her so she asked "Pick up your what"

18. "What do you need to pick up" Cathy asked again "Was it your books jeans shoes "

19. "Are you deaf " I asked I was getting tired of Cathy shouting so I started to leave

20. "Where are you going " she yelled at me

21. "Out" I said angrily slamming the door behind me just as I heard her say "He's so hard to get along with recently"

22. I was sorry to slam the door on her but couldn't she see how annoying she was

23. "Well" Cathy said exasperated "That's the last time he'll slam the door on me I'm getting out of here and believe me I'll never speak to him again"

24. Deborah said "What's wrong with you two I'll bet you ten dollars that you do speak to him again What do you want to bet"

25. Cathy didn't bet she told Deborah that we'd just had a bad day then she added "Don't you ever have a bad day "

2.5 Key to Exercises

1. I wanted to go for a hike and a swim, but Deborah was visiting and wouldn't leave.

    Statement calls for a comma and a period.

2. "Do you want to go for a hike and a swim with Cathy and me?" I asked her.

    This direct question calls for a question mark. Notice it is inside the quotation marks.

3. "How long do you think you'll be gone?" she asked.

    This is a direct question and calls for a question mark.

4. We told her we'd be gone for about three hours but wanted to know when she had to be back.

    This is an indirect question. The sentence only reports a question; it does not ask a question, so it does not call for a question mark. This is also a complex sentence, therefore, no comma is needed before *but*.

5. "Oh, about four p.m." she said, "Is that okay?"

    The sentence calls for a period after the abbreviation, *p.m.* Remember that *Oh* is parenthetical, so a comma follows it. A comma also follows *said*, because it leads into a quotation.

6. "Why that soon?" Cathy asked.

    This is a direct question and calls for a question mark.

7. "I have to call Mr. Shaw about the plumbing in my dorm and write a letter to Prof. Crosby about my paper that is due next week for my 9 a.m. class."

    Mr. and *Prof.* and *a.m.* call for periods, because they are abbreviations.

8. I asked her if there was a problem with her paper.

    This indirect question calls for a period.

9. "No," she replied, "but Prof. Crosby, Prof. Johnson, and Prof. Conner, etc., all assigned the same due date for their papers. Can you believe that? Don't they ever talk to one another?"

    In all three cases, the abbreviation *Prof.* calls for a period, as does *etc.* If the sentence read "But Profs. Crosby, Johnson, and Conner, *etc*...." You would punctuate it after the *s* in *Profs.* The last two direct questions call for question marks.

10. I wondered whether Deborah would have a hard time getting all the papers in on the same day.

    This sentence contains an indirect question; therefore, no question mark is needed.

11. "Maybe you could ask Prof. Crosby for an extension. He's pretty reasonable, isn't he?"

    This sentence contains one indirect question, punctuated with a period, and one direct question, punctuated with a question mark.

12. "I was thinking of that," she said. "Do you think he would mind?"

    Here, a quotation is interrupted by *she said.* Follow the quotation with a comma. We also have a quotation phrased as a direct question, which calls for a question mark.

13. Cathy wasn't listening, so she asked, "Who are you talking about?"

    A sentence is followed by a direct question. Two commas and a question mark inside the quotation mark are needed.

14. Deborah told her never mind, then asked when we were leaving for a hike.

An indirect statement and an indirect question. Follow the statement with a comma and place a period at the end of the sentence.

15. "What time do you want to leave?" I asked her.

    A direct question calls for a question mark.

16. "Right now," she said, then asked whether we could stop and pick up her books, her jeans, and her jogging shoes on the way.

    An indirect question calls for a period. Notice the comma after the introductory quotation.

17. Cathy didn't hear her, so she asked, "Pick up your what?"

    This direct question calls for a question mark. Notice the comma before *so* (the conjunction).

18. "What do you need to pick up?" Cathy asked again. "Was it your books, jeans, and shoes?"

    These two direct questions call for question marks. Actually, you have some flexibility here. You could punctuate the second question this way: Was it your books? Jeans? Shoes?

19. "Are you deaf?" I asked. I was getting tired of Cathy shouting, so I started to leave.

    This direct question calls for a question mark. A statement—in a compound sentence—calls for a period.

20. "Where are you going?" she yelled at me.

    This direct question calls for a question mark.

21. "Out!" I said angrily, slamming the door behind me just as I heard her say, "He's so hard to get along with recently."

    The first word is surely an exclamation, since it is said angrily. The second quotation makes a statement, which calls for a period.

22. I was sorry to slam the door on her, but couldn't she see how annoying she was?

    The compound sentence is a question, which calls for a question mark.

23. "Well!" Cathy said, exasperated. "That's the last time he'll slam the door on me! I'm getting out of here, and believe me, I'll never speak to him again!"

    The first sentence contains a comment—*Well!*— spoken in an exasperated tone of voice. This calls for an exclamation point. If it is assumed that the next two sentences are also spoken in exclamation, two more exclamation points are called for. Notice that the parenthetical words, *and believe me,* are set off with commas.

24. Deborah said, "What's wrong with you two? I'll bet you ten dollars that you do speak to him again. What do you want to bet?"

    This example contains two direct questions interrupted by one statement. Each direct question requires its own question mark and the statement requires a period.

25. Cathy didn't bet. She told Deborah that we'd just had a bad day, then she added: "Don't you ever have a bad day?"

    The first statement calls for a period. This is followed by a compound sentence—two independent clauses leading to a question. These are separated with a comma. A colon follows the final independent clause. Punctuate the question with a question mark.

See, isn't this fun! In the Chapter 3 you will learn about the magic of the semicolon.

Semicolons and Colons

: — ; / • , ? ! " " ' ( ) - ;

3

*A comma...catches the gentle drift of the mind
in thought, turning in on itself and back on
itself, reversing, redoubling, and returning along
the course of its own sweet river music; while the
semicolon brings clauses and thoughts together
with all the silent discretion of a hostess
arranging guests around her dinner table.*

—Pico Iyer

Without putting too fine a point on it, think of a semicolon
as an amber light on your highway to learning how to punctuate better. This is a caution light and it signifies that something
is going to happen. What happens is one of four things.

3.1 Joining Independent Clauses or Sentences

If your independent clauses are **closely related**—and you
could logically use a period to separate them—use a semicolon
instead. A sneaky way to think of semicolons is that they sometimes function as periods do.

Examples:

- Many philosophers have inspired; some have despaired.

- It's not too hot in here; it's not too cold either.

- I wouldn't say that Disneyland is the most exciting place I've ever been; I wouldn't say it's totally boring either.

- It's hard to know what the people in Washington are doing; they speak to us only through their public relations staff members.

- A semicolon is a complicated little mark; use it sparingly and with flair.

3.2 Making Transitions

Semicolons join sentences when you want to use transitional elements like *furthermore, moreover, likewise, meanwhile, thus.*

Using semicolons helps you move quickly from one idea to another idea or subject (*I will read your paper tonight; meanwhile, read chapter two of your textbook),* or to point out a contrast in the two sentences that you conjoin (*I like red; on the other hand, I think I like blue better.*).

Think of semicolons as linking ideas together when you want to make a transition in thought.

Examples:

- Cathy had a date; however, she would prefer having dinner with her women friends.

- Elizabeth was sick; otherwise, she would have come.

- Deborah looked in her closet and found nothing to wear; therefore, she decided to stay home.

- Michael was angry with Cathy for forgetting to feed the dog; moreover, he was upset about seeing her junk all over the table.

The sentences above are linked by *conjunctive adverbs.* There are a horrifying number of these, but when you understand how they operate, you'll recognize them.

Conjunctive Adverbs

also	namely
anyway	nevertheless
besides	next
certainly	now
finally	otherwise
however	similarly
incidentally	then
indeed	still
instead	therefore
meanwhile	thus
moreover	undoubtedly

There is also a terrifying glut of *transitional phrases*:

Transitional Phrases

as a consequence	in other words
as a result	in summary
as soon as	in the meantime
for example	of course
for instance	on the other hand
in fact	on the whole

These also link two sentences together. When they are located between two independent clauses they are preceded by a semicolon and followed by a comma.

Tip The basic thing to remember is that these word clusters are transitions: they move you quickly from one thought to the next in your writing.

Examples:

- She studied hard; as a result, she passed the test.

- She loved reading suspense novels; therefore, she tried to write one herself.

- Elizabeth was dressed to go out; however, the phone call delayed her, and she missed her ride.

3.3 Linking Lists After a Colon

Semicolons link lists after a colon, when the lists have their own internal punctuation.

Examples:

- On the highway, we passed a variety of cars: Fords, three black, one red; Chevrolets, two blues, three whites; Toyotas, one of each, black and red; Mazdas, two greens; and Volkswagens, one yellow.

- The banquet honored four of our students: Laura, who had the highest grade point average; Jonathan, who was the best all-round athlete; Pinky, who was the funniest person in class and drew the cartoons for the paper; and Caroline, who volunteered in the soup kitchen for the homeless.

You could write a new sentence for each of these people, but short, descriptive sentences can get monotonous. This, above, is a less boring, and more efficient way of writing about this related group of people. Why more efficient? It takes fewer words to describe these subjects when you set them up this way; it condenses the material but still gives each person equal attention.

3.4 Linking a Series

Semicolons join a short series of sentences or ideas. They help create that rhythm that you often depend on commas to do.

Examples:

- I came; I saw; I conquered.

- One flew East; one flew West; one flew over the cuckoo's nest.

- Ask not what your country can do for you; ask what you can do for your country.

- Guess who came to our party? Laura, who has interesting things to say; Jonathan, who just won the athletic award; Pinky, always entertaining; and Caroline, our conscience.

In all the cases above, you could start a new sentence to describe events or people. But if—for rhythm or style—you want to create closely knit sentences, use a semicolon.

 Tip Semicolons help writers to create parallelism—or a balance of words and thoughts—and to clarify the inner logic of their statements. That may sound theoretical, but actually, once you get the hang of it, you'll find semicolons are helpful little marks. It's not an accident that, visually, a semicolon is a period stacked on top of a comma. This makes it elegant. This gives it a bit of sophistication. This tells you: I am a complicated little mark; use me sparingly and with flair.

Examples:

- It's not just a job; it's an adventure.

- He was tall in stature, ruddy of face, sharp of feature; he was also generous of nature.

The semicolon is stronger than a comma—a green light—but less strong than a period—a red light. Thus, it's an amber light: it creates a pause between the green and red, so you can look to see what's about to happen. Often it keeps readers alert—keeps them from being bored with flat, simple sentences.

3.5 Exercises

Place punctuation where it is necessary.

1. Many people read novels others prefer nonfiction.

2. The semicolon is a period over a comma in its form you can see its function.

3. Living in a small town has many advantages however we have chosen the excitement of living in the city.

4. Health experts say that exercise extends your life indeed it may help you live to be one hundred years old.

5. The teacher urged the students to use the library for research nevertheless many of them used the Internet instead.

6. An advertiser sent me a fax I didn't want I simply dropped it in the wastebasket by my desk.

7. Florida was a perfect vacation site for our group: Cathy a world-class swimmer swam in the pool at the hotel Melissa snorkeled in the ocean Elizabeth who wanted to get away from the crowd went deep-sea fishing off the coast and Deborah lay around on the beach in a tiny bikini.

8. We enjoyed our trip to Aspen too because everyone could do what he or she wanted to: Michael who liked to ski was up at dawn Elizabeth who liked to hang out found new friends in the lounge Deborah the shopper in the crowd found lots of places to pursue her hobby and Cathy who has been known to sleep even on a subway slept.

9. Our crowd likes to hang out together therefore we often take vacations as a group.

10. The writer got tired of Elizabeth Deborah Cathy and Melissa as a result she began writing about Susan Calvin Whitney and David who were much more interesting.

11. The banker left a large estate therefore Susan his daughter who lives in Vermont Calvin his son who has a home in Atlanta Whitney his niece who lives in Houston and David a nephew who also lives in Texas inherited a great deal of money.

12. "You must be dreaming " declared Whitney "I never inherited a penny from that banker "

13. David chimed in "You've got to be kidding I never inherited a penny either otherwise I would be out of here "

14. Whitney a singer has performed in a number of musicals nevertheless her favorite is still Irving Berlin's *Annie Get Your Gun.*

15. David said "Here's a good slogan: work when you play play when you work "

16. Both David and Whitney were bright diligent determined and they worked hard in school as a result they both got into very good colleges.

17. Whitney is saving her money to go to Paris in the meantime she visits New York City on her spring breaks from school.

18. Whitney had a plan: She wanted to go with her friends Courtney Molly and Jennifer who loved the theater to all the plays on Broadway on the other hand David wanted to go to Cooperstown New York to see the Baseball Hall of Fame.

19. The people who won the awards were as follows: Tony for best drama Oscar for best film and Emmy for best television show

20. Grammy won an award for best music of the year but she was pretty old and didn't feel like dancing therefore she did not go to the award ceremony.

21. David said "Come play a computer game with me" of course Grammy would rather play music.

22. Susan and Calvin were bicycling uphill for almost an hour finally they got tired and stopped for a rest by the side of the road.

23. Calvin wrote an excellent research paper on Voltaire undoubtedly he would receive an A.

24. Susan called Grammy to play Scrabble however Grammy had gotten her energy back and was dancing.

25. Whitney called "Let's go for a ride in the Jeep "
    Meanwhile Wendy was backing out of the driveway in her
    little white Miata.

3.6 Key to Exercises

1. Many people read novels; others prefer nonfiction.
   A semicolon joins two independent clauses.

2. The semicolon is a period over a comma; in its form you
   can see its function.
   A semicolon again joins two independent clauses.

3. Living in a small town has many advantages; however, we
   have chosen the excitement of living in the city.
   A semicolon before a conjunctive adverb followed
   by a comma connects two independent clauses.

4. Health experts say that exercise extends your life; indeed,
   it may help you live to be one hundred years old.
   A semicolon before a conjunctive adverb followed
   by a comma connects two independent clauses.

5. The teacher urged the students to use the library for
   research; nevertheless, many of them used the Internet
   instead.
   A semicolon before a conjunctive adverb followed
   by a comma connects two independent clauses.

6. An advertiser sent me a fax I didn't want; I simply
   dropped it in the wastebasket by my desk.
   A semicolon joins two related independent clauses.

7. Florida was a perfect vacation site for our group: Cathy, a
   world-class swimmer, swam in the pool at the hotel;
   Melissa snorkeled in the ocean; Elizabeth, who wanted to
   get away from the crowd, went deep-sea fishing off the
   coast; and Deborah lay around on the beach in a tiny
   bikini.

Semicolons link a list that has its own internal punctuation to separate the list and make the sentence clearer. Notice that the list is introduced by a colon, not a semicolon.

8. We enjoyed our trip to Aspen, too, because everyone could do what he or she wanted to: Michael, who liked to ski, was up at dawn; Elizabeth, who liked to hang out, found new friends in the lounge; Deborah, the shopper in the crowd, found lots of places to pursue her hobby; and Cathy, who has been known to sleep even on a subway, slept.

Semicolons link items in a series with its own internal punctuation.

9. Our crowd likes to hang out together; therefore, we often take vacations as a group.

A semicolon is used before a conjunctive adverb, which is followed by a comma.

10. The writer got tired of Elizabeth, Deborah, Cathy, and Melissa; as a result, she began writing about Susan, Calvin, Whitney, and David, who are more interesting.

Notice here that we have words in a series without internal punctuation. So commas are used here instead of semicolons. The semicolon comes just before the transitional phrase, *as a result,* which is followed by a comma.

11. The banker left a large estate; therefore, Susan, his daughter, who lives in Vermont; Calvin, his son, who has a home in Atlanta; Whitney, his niece, who lives in Houston; and David, a nephew, who also lives in Texas, inherited the money.

A semicolon here comes before the conjunctive adverb, *therefore.* Also semicolons are used to separate words in a series that have their own internal punctuation. Remember appositives? Renaming the subject? Here, for example, Susan is the same person as the daughter, so we indicate that by setting the appositive off with a pair of commas. This sentence has several appositives—Calvin/son, Whitney/niece, David/nephew—and would become very confusing without proper punctuation.

12. "You must be dreaming," declared Whitney; "I never inherited a penny from that banker."

The semicolon joins two sentences or independent clauses. Notice the comma after *dreaming*; I might have placed an exclamation point there—and at the end of the sentence as well. Whitney may have been excited when she said this, and if that's the idea you want to get across to your reader, put exclamation points there. I didn't, because the sentence says "declared Whitney," and a declaration is not necessarily an exclamation. See? You have some freedom of interpretation with punctuation.

13. David chimed in, "You've got to be kidding. I never inherited a penny either; otherwise, I would be out of here!"

The semicolon joins two sentences or independent clauses separated by the conjunctive adverb, *otherwise.* There is an exclamation point at the end of this sentence, because it seemed like an exclamation to me. If, however, this was your sentence, and you didn't want it to read as an exclamation, you could put a period at the end. Maybe you placed a semicolon between *kidding* and *I*, because you saw there were two complete sentences or independent clauses within this quotation. You would not have been wrong to do so. To keep the quotation clean and as simple as possible, I used only one semicolon. The more you work with punctuation and see the opportunities it gives you to control how your writing is perceived, the more fun you will have with these little marks.

14. Whitney, a singer, has performed in a number of musicals; nevertheless, her favorite is still Irving Berlin's *Annie Get Your Gun.*

Again use a semicolon before a conjunctive adverb and a comma after it. Notice that *Whitney* and *a singer* are the same person, so set off this appositive with commas.

15. David said, "Here's a good slogan: work when you play; play when you work."

A colon introduces this short bit of wisdom, because it is an independent clause, and a semicolon separates the two sentences that form a balance, or parallel. A comma goes after *said,* which leads into a direct quote. We will discuss further uses of the colon.

16. Both David and Whitney were bright, diligent, determined, and they worked hard in school; as a result, they both got into very good colleges.

Here the words in a series are short and have no internal punctuation, so commas separate them, rather than semicolons. The semicolon separates the first independent clause from the transitional phrase, *as a result,* and the second independent clause.

17. Whitney is saving her money to go to Paris; in the meantime, she visits New York City on her spring breaks from school.

Use a semicolon before a transitional phrase, which is followed by a comma.

18. Whitney had a plan: She wanted to go with her friends, Courtney, Molly, and Jennifer, who loved the theater, to all the plays on Broadway; on the other hand, David wanted to go to Cooperstown, New York, to see the Baseball Hall of Fame.

A colon was placed after *plan* because the words that follow tell what that plan was. *She* was capitalized, because all the words that come after it constitute a complete sentence. If you used a colon, and the words just after it are a list, or otherwise not a complete sentence, the first word should not be capitalized. The semicolon separates the first independent clause from the transitional phrase and the second independent clause. *On the other hand* could have begun a new sentence. But hey! We're studying semicolons, and the more you see how they work, the better.

19. The people who won the awards were as follows: Tony, for best drama; Oscar, for best film; and Emmy, for best television show.

    When you see the words *as follows*, you can bet a list will follow it, so put a colon after the phrase. Here the semicolons separate words in a series with their own internal punctuation.

20. Grammy won an award for best music of the year, but she was pretty old and didn't feel like dancing; therefore, she did not go to the award ceremony.

    The semicolon belongs before the conjunctive adverb and the comma belongs after. Notice the comma before *but*, which conjoins two independent clauses.

21. David said, "Come play a computer game with me"; of course, Grammy would rather play music.

    Here you see something new: the semicolon is placed **outside** the quotation mark. Can you guess why? Yes, it's because the punctuation is not a part of the quotation. It simply separates the quotation from the transitional phrase and the rest of the sentence. Remember that periods and commas go inside the quotation marks. Semicolons, question marks, and exclamation points can sometimes go **outside**; it all depends on the structure and sense of the sentence. You'll see some more examples in Chapter 5.

22. Susan and Calvin were bicycling uphill for almost an hour; finally, they got tired and stopped for a rest by the side of the road.

    Again, the semicolon is used before the conjunctive adverb, which is followed by a comma.

23. Calvin wrote an excellent research paper on Voltaire; undoubtedly, he would receive an A.

    A semicolon is used before a conjunctive adverb, which is followed by a comma.

24. Susan called Grammy to play Scrabble; however, Grammy had gotten her energy back and was dancing.

    Again, a semicolon is used before a conjunctive adverb, which is followed by a comma.

25. Whitney yelled, "Let's go for a ride in the Jeep!" Meanwhile, Wendy was backing out of the driveway in her little white Miata.

    Okay, here's something new. You'll notice Whitney is yelling; therefore, the exclamation point goes **inside the quotation mark** because the punctuation is a part of her yell. The sentence would be cluttered if we put a semicolon here, although *meanwhile* is certainly a conjunctive adverb. So, to make your sentence read smoothly and simply, divide this into two sentences. All conjunctive adverbs do not have to be preceded by semicolons. They may open sentences as well—then they are seen as introductory elements and should be followed by a comma. All clear? Don't worry, sometimes punctuation can become complicated, but if you understand the basics, you'll learn how to use it well.

3.7 Colons

A colon draws you up short, keeps you alert, signals that something is coming up, so watch for it. It tells the reader that a list will follow, or that something promised or hinted at will be delivered, or that a series of items or a quotation is to follow. Colons also have several more technical uses that we will examine here.

▶ **Use a colon after an independent clause to tell the reader that a list will follow.**

Examples:

- She brought her school supplies to class: notebooks, pens, and textbooks.

- He learned the three secrets of buying real estate: location, location, and location.

- His music teacher told him how to get to Carnegie Hall: practice, practice, practice.

▶ **Use a colon to introduce something that the independent clause preceding it has promised but has not yet delivered.**

Examples:

- We finally understood why we couldn't communicate: He talked too much, and I talked too much.

Colon delivers material hinted at previously.

- Wandering in Paris, she suddenly understood what she needed: a guidebook.

Colon delivers the answer to the question the reader has after reading the words before it.

▶ **Use a colon before a series of items or a quotation.**

Examples:

- As we put the program together, we asked ourselves: Who is the audience? What do they want to know? How many will come? How do we keep their attention?

The colon indicates that a series of items is to follow.

- "Was it Sydney Carton in *A Tale of Two Cities* who said this: 'Tis a far, far better thing I do now than I have ever done'?"

After an independent clause, a colon is often used to lead into a direct quotation. Notice the punctuation here: Single quotation marks surround the quotation within a quotation. *'Tis* is a contraction of *it is*, so it takes an apostrophe. The question mark lies outside the single quotation mark, because the question is asked within the full sentence, not within the single quotation.

- The sign on the food store read: "Ample parking in back."

A colon may be used to lead into a direct quotation.

Other Uses of a Colon

▶ **To separate elements.**

For example, **salutations** in a letter to someone you do not know very well—a formal letter.

Dear Mr. Downhill:	Dear Dr. Overhill:
Dear Ms. Uphill:	Dear Reverend Underhill:

Hours and Minutes

Examples:

7:15	12:45	3:10

Ratios
Examples:
a ratio of 12:1   a slim margin of 6:5

▶ **Titles and Subtitles**

Examples:
- "The Turn of the Screw": A Study of the Supernatural
- *Plain English: The Joy of Writing Clearly*

▶ **Biblical Chapters and Verses**

Examples:
Genesis 2:6-9   Matthew 5:27   Luke 4:31-44

▶ **Bibliographical Entries—cities and publishers**

Examples:
- New York: Random House, 2001
- Boston: Little, Brown, 1998

 Tip) Except for separating elements, don't use a colon after a sentence fragment. If you are tempted to do that, rewrite the sentence.

For example:

Don't: "She came to class with: notebooks, pens, and textbooks."

Do: "She brought her school supplies to class: notebooks, pens, and textbooks."

Remember this general rule:

If a full sentence comes after your colon, capitalize the first letter in that sentence. If a list or a fragment comes after your colon, do not capitalize the first word.

3.8 Exercises

Supply all necessary punctuation in the sentences below.

1. She checked her travel bag for everything she needed for her trip to Rome passport plane ticket wallet money phone numbers hotel reservation and map

2. Jerry said please write down what I need from the supermarket milk juice bread bananas peanut butter

3. Morris drafted the cover letter for his job application Dear Mr Rich he wrote Enclosed please find my application and resume for the position of Marketing Assistant for which you advertised

4. Jean's term paper was titled Arthur Miller's Short Story Bulldog The Author's Use of Metaphor

5. It was clear to me why I did not make the Honor Roll I had four A's one B and one C.

6. In the composition class we studied grammar syntax and basic mechanics of writing

7. In the second class we studied the following how to research a subject write a thesis statement support the thesis and come to a conclusion

8. Hugh visited several dealerships and found three kinds of cars he wanted to buy Cadillac BMW Jaguar

9. Arent you aiming a little high asked his father I was thinking more on the order of Ford Chevrolet Toyota

10. For our study of the Bible we were asked to read I Corinthians 15 58

11. For one citation in her bibliography Susan wrote Woodward, C. Vann. ed. *Mary Chesnut's Civil War.* New Haven, Conn. Yale University Press, 1981.

12. The group told me to meet them at The Museum of Natural History at 1 15 unfortunately the bus moved slowly through the traffic and I didnt get there until 1 30 by that time they had already gone inside

13. The ratio of men to women in our class of twenty students was 4 1

14. In my immediate family we have birthdays in the following months January (1) February (2) March April and May (1 each) and July (4).

15. From *The New York Times Manual of Style and Usage:* Today is the dead center of the year or as near dead center as one can conveniently get 182 days gone by 182 to come.

16. One rule for using colons is this Capitalize the initial letter after the colon if it introduces a complete sentence do not capitalize it if it is a fragment

17. When considering a college here are some questions to ask does it have a good reputation can I afford it does it offer a strong department in the area I want to study is it in a location of the country where I want to live

18. Wise words about honoring parents can be found in the Bible in Matthew 15 4 in addition wise words about patience can be found in Hebrews 10 36

19. For my grandfather's seventy fifth birthday he got everything he wanted a new reclining chair four new books and season tickets to the Yankees

20. I knew what the professor was about to say please bring your portfolio to class next Tuesday

21. At the barbeque this is what we had to eat beans potato salad deviled eggs peach cobbler and oh yes barbeque

22. I turned in my paper titled The Sermons of Martin Luther King An Analysis unfortunately my professor said it was long on Dr. King's sermons and short on my analysis so I had to revise it

23. The reviewer said Henry's book had these remarkable traits depth clarity and excellent use of research

24. In the story the narrator reveals a variety of contradictory fears fear of being alone and fear of commitment fear that his extreme discipline had made him stuffy and fear of losing control

25. One train leaves Penn Station at 10 42 p m and the next at 12 01 a m

3.9 Key to Exercises

1. She checked her travel bag for everything she needed for her trip to Rome: passport, plane ticket, wallet, money, phone numbers, hotel reservations, and map.

2. Jerry said, "Please write down what I need from the supermarket: milk, juice, bananas, peanut butter."

3. Morris drafted the cover letter for his job application: "Dear Mr. Rich," he wrote. "Enclosed please find my application and resume for the position of Marketing Assistant for which you advertised."

    Morris could correctly write "Dear Mr. Rich:" too—depending on how formal he wishes to be. A colon after the salutation is more formal than a comma.

4. Jean's term paper was titled "Arthur Miller's Short Story, 'Bulldog': The Author's Use of Metaphor."

    Jean would not put the quotation marks around the title of her paper that she planned to turn in to the teacher. But this sentence simply reports on Jean's term paper, so it should be punctuated the way it is here.

5. It was clear to me why I did not make the Honor Roll: I had four *A*'s, one *B*, and one *C*.

6. In the composition class, we studied grammar, syntax, and basic mechanics of writing.

7. In the second class, we studied the following: how to research a subject, write a thesis statement, support the thesis, and come to a conclusion.

    The material following the colon is not a complete sentence, so don't capitalize it.

8. Hugh visited several dealerships and found three kinds of cars he wanted to buy: Cadillac, BMW, Jaguar.

9. "Aren't you aiming a little high?" asked his father. "I was thinking more on the order of Ford, Chevrolet, and Toyota."

10. For our study of the Bible, we were asked to read I
    Corinthians 15:58.

    You would not generally put I Corinthians 15:58 in
    quotation marks, even though it is a book within a book.
    This is simply a convention we use. Example of a further
    convention: "I was asked to read a biblical passage in
    class." Generally, we do not capitalize or italicize biblical.

11. For one citation in her bibliography, Susan wrote:
    Woodward, C. Vann. ed., *Mary Chesnut's Civil War.* New
    Haven, Conn.: Yale University Press, 1981.

    When writing citations for research papers, be sure
    to check with your teacher to find out what stylebook
    he or she prefers that you follow.

12. The group told me to meet them at The Museum of
    Natural History at 1:15; unfortunately, the bus moved
    slowly through the traffic, and I didn't get there until 1:30.
    By that time they had already gone inside.

    Notice that this example contains three full sen-
    tences. You can punctuate them with periods or use one
    semicolon and one period. It is a little awkward to have
    more than one semicolon in a sentence when you are
    punctuating independent clauses.

13. The ratio of men to women in our class of twenty students
    was 4:1.

14. In my immediate family, we have birthdays in the
    following months: January (1); February (2); March,
    April, and May (1 each); and July (4).

15. From *The New York Times Manual of Style and Usage:*
    "Today is the dead center of the year or as near dead
    center as one can conveniently get: 182 days gone by, 182
    to come."

16. One rule for using colons is this: Capitalize the initial letter after the colon if it introduces a complete sentence; do not capitalize it if it is a fragment.

17. When considering a college, here are some questions to ask: Does it have a good reputation; can I afford it; does it offer a strong department in the area I want to study; is it in a location of the country where I want to live?

    You could also separate all of these questions with a question mark and capitalize the initial letter of each question: Does it have a good reputation? Can I afford it? *etc.*

18. Wise words about honoring parents can be found in the Bible in Matthew 15:4; in addition, wise words about patience can be found in Hebrews 10:36.

19. For my grandfather's seventy-fifth birthday, he got everything he wanted: a new reclining chair, four new books, and season tickets to the Yankees.

20. I knew what the professor was about to say: "Please bring your portfolio to class next Tuesday."

21. At the barbeque, this is what we had to eat: beans, potato salad, deviled eggs, peach cobbler, and barbeque.

    You may have chosen to set off "oh yes" in parentheses or with commas, both of which are correct. I chose this punctuation to give the sentence a little tag word.

22. I turned in my paper titled "The Sermons of Martin Luther King: An Analysis"; unfortunately, my professor said it was long on Dr. King's sermons and short on my analysis, so I had to revise it.

    In speaking of a paper, it is appropriate to put its title in quotation marks. A student would not do so at the top of the page of her actual paper.

23. The reviewer said Henry's book had these remarkable traits: depth, clarity, and excellent use of research.

24. In the story, the narrator reveals a variety of contradictory fears: fear of being alone, and fear of commitment; fear that his extreme discipline had made him stuffy, and fear of losing control.

25. One train leaves Penn Station at 10:42 p.m. and the next at 12:01 a.m.

    If the last part of this sentence had read "and the next train leaves at 12:01 a.m.," you would have placed a comma after "p.m." because it would then be a compound sentence—not complex, as it is now.

4

Apostrophes

: — ; / • , ? ! " " ' ( ) - ;

> *"That little airborne mark that dangles over
> some words (including last names like
> O'Conner) is called an apostrophe. This is
> the punctuation mark that has many sign
> painters mystified. Store awnings and windows,
> sides of trucks, even neon signs are peppered
> with wayward apostrophes that either don't
> belong at all or are in the wrong position."*
>
> —Patricia T. O'Conner, Editor

After the elegant semicolon, you are going to think that working with the prosaic apostrophe is a piece of cake. There are only three basic kinds of apostrophes: the contraction apostrophe, the possessive apostrophe, and the plural apostrophe. There *is* also the exceptional apostrophe, but if you pay attention and do the exercises in sequence, you'll learn all the types quickly.

4.1 Contractions

This apostrophe mark (') takes the place of letters that have been dropped out of a word for one reason or another. Sometimes letters are dropped out to make the language more conversational:

> I'll be around after you're gone.

(More formally: I will be around after you are gone.) Here, you have dropped out the *w* in *will* and the *a* in *are*. These new word formations are called **contractions**.

> Who's going skating with me?

(More formally: Who is going skating with me?)

> I won't dance; don't ask me.

Here the contraction for *will not* is *won't*. *Won't* is easier to speak than *willn't*, the true contraction, so in English language usage, we have come to accept this as the convention. You may find the *willn't* contraction in some 19th Century prose, especially British prose, but in common American English we *don't*—do not—ordinarily use it.

> "I am goin' to fix my bike with the broken wheel and the danglin' light," Charlie said.

(More formally: I am going to fix my bike with the broken wheel and the dangling light.) When you are writing dialogue, you may want to make your language sound colloquial—conversational and informal.

Remember to put the apostrophe in the exact place that the letters are dropped, and if you drop two or more letters, you'll need two or more apostrophes. For example, no matter what you see on T-shirts or in advertisements, when you want to write *rock and roll* informally, you should write *rock 'n' roll* to be correct, because you've dropped out two letters—*a* and *d*.

4.2 Possessives

This apostrophe shows possession or ownership. There are several sub-rules that make ownership a little complicated.

The simple rule is this:

If the noun is singular, simply add an apostrophe *s*— even to those that already end in *s*.

Examples

- Matthew's house is strung with lights for Christmas.
- John's horse got away and ended up in Norman's pasture.
- Rufus's motor home was in the park ground.
- The bus's motor was noisy, but the car's was not.

But the following usage may seem a little puzzling to you

The ring's disappearance caused her to cry.

I know, I know. The ring does not actually own its disappearance. This is a loose interpretation of ownership, but the apostrophe is placed correctly.

Her brother's absence from the table delayed dinner.

Again, this is a loose kind of ownership. Another way to state this is *The absence of her brother from the table delayed dinner,* in the same way that you might say *The house of her brother has a new roof.* In this sense, her brother owns the absence in much the same way that he owns the house. The rule is a little fast and loose, but that's it.

4.3 Plurals

Now, things get even more complicated: **If the noun is plural and an *s* has already been added, put an apostrophe after the *s* that is already there:**

> The houses' rafters had been strung with lights for Christmas.

This statement assumes that there is more than one house strung with lights.

▶ **If a name ends in s, like Gillies, the plural adds es (the Gillieses), and the possessive adds an apostrophe (the Gillieses' barn).**

> The Marcuses' house, next door to the Rosses' house, has also been strung with lights.

This assumes two or more people own, or inhabit, the Marcus house and the Ross house.

 Tip If the Millers or the Smiths have name signs on their houses, these signs should read The Millers or The Smiths. (This means that the Millers or Smiths live here.) The signs should not contain apostrophes.

Some nouns are irregular, meaning they change forms when they indicate two or more: like man, men; woman, women; alumnus, alumni. (Did I tell you this was simple? Sorry.) In this case, since the noun has already been made plural by a different spelling, treat it as if it were singular.

Examples:

- The men's hats were taken by the hatcheck and placed in the closet.
- The women's coats hung in a separate closet.

- The alumni's tickets were held at the college box office.
- The geese's eggs lay at the edge of the pond.

▶ **If you are using a *pronoun* that is already possessive, do not add an apostrophe.**

Examples:

- His hat was taken by the hatcheck and placed in the closet.
- Her coat hung in a separate closet.
- Their tickets were held at the college box office.
- Your geese are sitting on my geese's eggs!
- The house is yours, the barn is mine, the car is his, and the property is theirs.
- Its bone is next to its bowl.

 Tip) Please remember this: *Its* is the possessive form of it—referring to inanimate objects, animals, and babies whose gender you do not know:

Examples:

- The baby dropped *its* rattle.
- *Its* saddle and halter are in the barn.
- The radio has lost *its* sound.
- The TV has lost *its* picture.

Do not confuse this with *it's*—the contraction of *it is*—in which the second *i* has been dropped.

It's (it is) a long, long way to Tipperary. It's (it is) a long way to go. It's (it is) an old, old song.

> ❱ **Indefinite pronouns—someone, anyone, everyone—take an apostrophe *s* to become posessive.**

Examples:

- Anyone's guess is a good as mine.
- Someone's car is in my driveway.
- Everyone's name is on the guest list.

4.4 The Exceptional Apostrophe

Single letters, numbers, symbols, and words used as terms look awkward when written as plurals without any punctuation, so we generally add an apostrophe *s* to them.

Examples:

- There are two *a*'s in the word "separate."
- His grades are all in the high *90*'s.
- Can you change this 10 for two *5*'s?
- He lived in the *1960*'s; I live in the *2000*'s.

 Tip There is another way of treating the exceptional apostrophe. Letters, numbers, symbols, and words used as terms can also be set off from the text by merely adding an s.

Examples:

- Always cross your Ts.
- We will set the theme for the party by playing music from the 60s.
- Remember to capitalize all the CIAs in your report.

▶ **To abbreviate years and add the plural, use an apostrophe and add s.**

Example:
> He lived in the '60s; I live in the '90s.

▶ **When discussing symbols in the plural, do it this way:**
> "Please insert ^'s when you see a word has been left out," the editor said.

 Tip When you write letters, numbers, symbols, *etc.*, as above, you should italicize them, but do not italicize the plural endings—'s.

Examples:
- He wrote $'s in his note, rather than spelling out the word.
- The editor instructed: "When you write &'s, you are writing more than one *and*; the symbol is called an ampersand."

We will discuss italics more fully in a later chapter.

4.5 Exercises

Write the following sentences using apostrophes, adding the proper punctuation, and forming contractions.

1. "Whats going on here" John asked.

_____

_____

_____

_____

2. Dont let this little disturbance bother you Youll feel better very soon.

_____

_____

_____

3. Youll find a way to make this work I assure you Just dont get upset about something that you cant change

_____

_____

_____

4. He told me that working for Iztec isnt all its cracked up to be.

_____

_____

5. Hes taller than she is certainly but shes developed a lot of upper body strength.

_____

_____

_____

6. You wouldnt think it when looking outside but the weather forecaster said wed have snow tomorrow. (Use your common sense here, then check the answer key.)

_____

_____

_____

7. I said "Dont do it! This wont be good for you or your family" but John wouldnt listen and the project was a disaster.

_____

_____

_____

_____

8. Lets find time to play lets find time to work lets find time to be with our friends.

_____

_____

_____

9. The space is large enough to back my car into isnt it?

_____

_____

10. The Eganses property is next door to the Carpenters property but the Eganses place is larger and doesnt have so many outbuildings on it however the Carpenters place is easier to manage.

_____

_____

_____

_____

_____

_____

11. Tim and Jays dog got away and ran into the next-door neighbors yard but the neighbors were good about it and didnt appear upset.

_____

_____

_____

_____

_____

12. Ever since the flood the windows need to be washed on all the houses peoples roofs need to be repaired and their doors rehung.

_____

_____

_____

_____

13. The earths surface looks very different from outer space than it looks here however we think our view of the earth is normal.

_____

_____

_____

_____

_____

14. The Williamses swimming pool has algae in it because they have been away all summer and havent had anyone to take care of the pool.

_____

_____

_____

_____

15. I told the delivery man to put all the new furniture in the kids room because they need new beds and chests unfortunately the men put the kids beds in the wrong room so I will have to hire someone to move it.

_____

_____

_____

_____

_____

_____

16. The mens and womens rooms were side by side in the restaurant however I walked into the wrong one and I will never get over my embarrassment!

_____

_____

_____

_____

17. It isnt a good time to plant flowers now because the
    ground is still frozen and they will not root in this
    temperature.

_____

_____

_____

_____

_____

18. I wanted to give the waiter a tip but I had only two 20s so
    I asked the cashier for some change which was the only
    thing I knew to do but she had no change finally I asked
    another man in the restaurant and he gave me four 10s so
    I gave the waiter one.

_____

_____

_____

_____

_____

_____

_____

19. "What" she screamed "Youre going home without me"

_____

_____

_____

20. My mom told me that after the 1960s there were a lot of cultural changes in this country so new laws that affected minorities and women were put into effect.

_____

_____

_____

_____

_____

21. I wrote to my father: "We can't use $'s when we are shopping in London however we often take pounds with us so we're assured of having what we need to hire a taxi to get from the airport."

_____

_____

_____

_____

_____

_____

22. During her first year in college she received four As and one B+ therefore her parents let her take a trip to Italy that summer.

_____

_____

_____

_____

23. Ours were good seats at the stadium but our friends didnt like theirs so they went back to exchange them.

_____

_____

_____

_____

24. The twins are like two peas in a pod: They wear identical clothes and both of them make As in school.

_____

_____

_____

_____

25. The cat lay on its stomach on the microwave because that was the warmest place in the house but the dog was playing with its bone outside and I thought if its going to get any colder I might have to get a heater for the babys room or shell freeze.

_____

_____

_____

_____

_____

_____

_____

4.6 Key to Exercises

1. "What's going on here?" John asked.

2. Don't let this little disturbance bother you. You'll feel better very soon.

3. You'll find a way to make this work, I assure you. Just don't get upset about something that you can't change.

4. He told me that working for Iztec isn't all it's cracked up to be.

5. He's taller than she is, certainly, but she's developed a lot of upper body strength.

   Notice that the first *she is* is not made into a contraction. In English we don't say "He's taller than she's." But we do say "She's developed a lot of upper body strength.

6. You wouldn't think it when looking outside, but the weather forecaster said we'd have snow tomorrow.

   Well, here's an exception. I told you to insert an apostrophe for each letter you drop. In this case, we would have to write *"we''''d* have snow." This looks pretty silly, which is probably the reason we don't do it. Contract *we would* to *we'd,* using only one apostrophe.

7. I said, "Don't do it! This won't be good for you or your family," but John wouldn't listen, and the project was a disaster.

8. Let's find time to play; let's find time to work; let's find time to be with our friends.

   These sentences are all closely related and parallel—that is, have the same subject and verb form and repeat words. Therefore, I connected them with semicolons. *Let's* is a contraction of *Let us.*

9. The space is large enough to back my car into, isn't it?

   Here you will notice an exception to the contraction and apostrophe rule. *Isn't it* literally is a contraction for *is not it*. In English, we use *isn't* as a contraction for *is not*. Why? Well, try to say a literal contraction for *is not it*. Sounds pretty much like a grunt, does it not? Likewise, *doesn't it* is the contraction for *does not it*. The negative—*not*—frequently demands that we make adjustments in contracting expressions and this, of course, affects apostrophe use.

10. The Eganses' property is next door to the Carpenters' property, but the Eganses' place is larger and doesn't have as many outbuildings on it; however, the Carpenters' place is easier to manage.

11. Tim and Jay's dog got away and ran into the next-door neighbor's yard, but the neighbors were good about it and didn't appear upset.

    Note that you don't need to say "Tim's and Jay's dog." The name closest to the possession carries the apostrophe because Tim and Jay both own the same dog. If Tim had his own dog and Jay had his own dog, the sentence would read *Tim's and Jay's dogs*.

12. Ever since the flood, the windows need to be washed on all the houses; people's roofs need to be repaired and their doors rehung.

    People is already plural, so you simply add apostrophe *s*. The two independent clauses are closely related, so I used a semicolon here.

13. The earth's surface looks very different from outer space than it looks here; however, we think our view of the earth is normal.

14. The Williamses' swimming pool has algae in it, because they have been away all summer and haven't had anyone to take care of the pool.

    That family's last name is Williams but the pool belongs to all the members of the family. For plural names ending in *s*, add only the apostrophe.

15. I told the delivery man to put all the new furniture in the kids' room, because they need new beds and chests; unfortunately, the men put the kids' beds in the wrong room, so I'll have to hire someone to move them.

    The plural possessive, *kids*, requires an apostrophe, *kids'*.

16. The men's and women's rooms were side by side in the restaurant; however, I walked into the wrong one, and I'll never get over my embarrassment!

    You could punctuate the ending here with either a period or an exclamation point, depending on how embarrassed you are! These plural possessive pronouns require an apostrophe s.

17. It isn't a good time to plant flowers now, because the ground is still frozen, and they'll not root in this temperature.

18. I wanted to give the waiter a tip, but I had only two *20*'s, so I asked the cashier for some change, which was the only thing I knew to do, but she had no change; finally, I asked another man in the restaurant, and he gave me four *10*'s, so I gave the waiter one.

    You could stop the sentence after *change* with a period and begin a new one with *Finally*. Either way is correct. Notice that the numerals are in italics.

19. "What!" she screamed. "You're going home without me?"

    Notice that the exclamation point and the question mark are both inside the quotation marks indicating that the exclamation and the question are being screamed and asked by the same speaker.

20. My mom told me that after the *1960*s there were a lot of cultural changes in this country, so many new laws that affect minorities and women were put into effect.

21. I wrote to my father: "We can't use *$*'s when we are shopping in London; however, we often take pounds with us, so we're assured of having what we need to hire a taxi to get from the airport."

    Notice the direct quotation is in proper marks here. The dollar symbol is in italics, but the s is not.

22. During her first year in college she received four *A*'s and one *B*+; therefore, her parents let her take a trip to Italy that summer.

    Italicize single letters, but do not italicize the s.

23. Ours were good seats at the stadium, but our friends didn't like theirs, so they went back to exchange them.

    Plural possessive pronouns—such as *ours*—do not take apostrophes.

24. The twins are like two peas in a pod: They wear identical clothes, and both of them make *A*'s in school.

25. The cat lay on its stomach on the microwave, because that was the warmest place in the house, but the dog was playing with its bone outside, and I thought, if it's going to get any colder, I might have to get a heater for the baby's room or she'll freeze.

This sentence might also be punctuated like this:

> The cat lay on its stomach on the microwave because that was the warmest place in the house, but the dog was playing with its bone outside, and I thought if it's going to get any colder I might have to get a heater for the baby's room or she'll freeze.

Remember that punctuation is about not confusing readers. There is really nothing in the above sentence—even though it is long—that is likely to be misread or to confuse the reader if some of the conventional commas were omitted. My advice is to learn and use conventional punctuation until you are so secure about the way to use it that you can make an informed judgment about omitting it in selected instances.

Quotation Marks

5

Punctuation, then, is a matter of care.

—Pico Iyer

Actually, quotation marks are used in only four basic ways, but there is much more to be said about them. For example: when **not** to use quotation marks, when to use single quotation marks, how to punctuate when using quotation marks, how to quote long and short passages of prose and verse. The *don't*s are as important as the *do*'s when you use these marks.

Let's start with the four ways to use them:

5.1 Direct Quotations

Examples:

- In *Alice in Wonderland,* Alice is repeatedly astonished by the strange things she sees. "Curiouser and curiouser!" she says on one occasion when she is so surprised that "she quite forgot how to speak good English."

- The prophet Isaiah in the Bible calls for preparations for the coming of the Lord by saying, "Make straight in the desert a highway for our God. Valleys will be raised up, the mountains leveled."

- In his novel *Catch-22*, Joseph Heller gives us a new way of phrasing "You're damned if you do, and you're damned if you don't": "Catch-22."

Notice you have two uses of quotations in the Heller allusion separated by a colon placed outside both quotations. Notice, too, that the final period goes within the quotation mark, though logic would tell you that it should go outside, since it closes the full sentence rather than the final quotation only. Just remember: periods and commas go inside quotation marks.

- Of death, William Shakespeare says in *Hamlet,* we "shuffle off this mortal coil."

Here we are quoting Shakespeare directly, so the final five words must be surrounded by quotation marks. If the sentence read thus: Of death, William Shakespeare says in *Hamlet* that we shuffle off this mortal coil, then we would be quoting indirectly and wouldn't need quotation marks. The *that* in the last sentence shifts the quotation to indirect.

 Tip When you are quoting or writing dialogue, start a new paragraph (indent) with every new speaker.

"Beauty is in the eye of the beholder."

"But I don't know what that means."

"It means, my dear, that beauty is not objective or inherent in the person described as beautiful. Rather, it is subjective—determined by the one who perceives it."

"Oh, well then, I think you are beautiful!"

5.2 Titles of Short Works

Articles, short stories, essays, songs, short poems, stage plays, titles of art work, and titles of films, television shows, and radio programs should be surrounded by quotation marks.

Examples:

- The women in the beauty salon were watching "Oprah," while their hair was being cut.

If you are speaking of Oprah as a person, you would not put her name in quotation marks.

- Who was *Time* magazine's "Man of the Year?"

The name of the magazine itself is italicized; the featured article is in quotation marks.

- John Keats said, "Beauty is truth, truth beauty," in his poem "Ode on a Grecian Urn."

Both the poem, because it is relatively short, and the specific quotation should be in quotation marks.

- The choir sang Handel's "Messiah."

 Tip) Actually, the oratorio is titled "The Messiah." But typically when you use the composer's or author's or writer's name before a work, you drop the article (a, an, the) before the title. Another example: The students presented Shakespeare's "Midsummer-Night's Dream." The actual title is "A Midsummer-Night's Dream." Drop the article "A."

- Mary saw "Venus de Milo" in the Louvre last May.

"Venus de Milo" is a sculpture.

Tip Some teachers may prefer film titles to be italicized: *All the President's Men*, for example. Italicizing, underlining, or placing works in quotation marks are relatively unimportant choices when writing. The basic thing to remember is to be consistent about how you treat each of these pieces of literature and art—and ask your teacher what he or she prefers.

5.3 Definitions and Words as Words

Examples:

- I can never remember how to spell "correspondent"; I want to put an "a" in the last syllable.

Here a word is used as a word.

- An aardvark is "a burrowing African mammal."

Here we are defining a word—"aardvark."

- Zymurgy is "the branch of chemistry dealing with fermentation, as applied in wine making and brewing."
- What does "dodecahedron" mean? It is "a solid figure with twelve plane faces"—used in geometry.

5.4 Ironic Distance

Examples:

- Is he your "significant other?"
- I didn't say I wasn't "interested." I just said I didn't want to get "involved."
- Well, look what being "a good student" has gotten me: more work!

5.5 Block Quotations

If the passage you want to quote is more than four typed lines, set it off by indenting it ten spaces from the left margin. It is commonly recommended to single space the quotation; however, there are style books that suggest double spacing (so check with your instructor). This is called a block quotation, and you do not place quotation marks around it. The indention itself serves as quotation marks.

Example:

> Other people, so I have read, measure memorable moments in their lives: the time one climbed the Parthenon at sunrise, the summer night one met a lonely girl in Central Park and achieved with her a sweet and natural relationship, as they say in books. I, too, once met a girl in Central Park, but it is not much to remember. What I remember is the time John Wayne killed three men with a carbine as he was falling to the dusty street in 'Stagecoach,' and the time the kitten found Orson Welles in the doorway in 'The Third Man.'
>
> —Walker Percy

If you use a block quotation, and you have quotations within the block, you should use single quotation marks around them. Notice the last two lines of the previous passage. Normally, you would put "Stagecoach" and "The Third Man" in double quotation marks (or italicize them). But the logic here is that a block format indicates a quotation itself, so you use single marks as you would with any quotation within a quotation.

You should use single quotation marks if you are quoting within a block quotation. If the line in the previous passage read this way, you would use single quotation marks:

> Walker Percy said, 'What I remember is the time John Wayne killed three men with a carbine.'

5.6 Quoting Poetry

When quoting up to and including three lines of poetry within a paper you are writing, incorporate it within the text you are writing, but separate the line of the poem with a space, slash, space to show where a line of poetry ends and the next one begins.

Example:

> No one can fail to respond to Lewis Carroll's sense of fun in his delightful poem, "Jabberwocky." It begins, "'Twas brillig, and the slithy tove / Did gyre and gimble in the wabe; / All mimsy were the borogoves, / And the mome raths outgrabe."
>
> In *Through the Looking Glass,* Alice and Humpty Dumpty discuss this nonsense poem, coming to no conclusion about what any of these words mean.

When you quote more than three lines of poetry, indent each line ten spaces and single space them. Do not use quotation marks. Treat it as you would treat a block quotation. And remember to keep the words and punctuation exactly as you found them in the original.

Example:

> Let us go then, you and I,
> When the evening is spread out against the sky
> Like a patient etherized upon a table;
> Let us go through certain half-deserted streets,
> The muttering retreats
> Of restless nights in one-night cheap hotels
> And sawdust restaurants with oyster-shells:...

—T. S. Eliot
from *The Love Song of J. Alfred Prufrock*

5.7 Big Don'ts

▶ **Don't use quotation marks around whole books, anthologies, newspapers, or magazines (underline or italicize them).**

Examples:

- *How a Poem Means*, by John Ciardi, is a charming and instructive read.
- *Newsweek, Time,* and *U.S. News and World Report* are weekly newsmagazines.
- *The New York Review of Books* is my favorite periodical.
- *The Norton Anthology of Poetry* is indispensable in any home library.

▶ **Don't use quotation marks around the titles of the papers you write.**

Examples:

- Sibling Rivalry: Lear's Daughters in "King Lear"
- Henry James' *Portrait of A Lady*: The Author's Symbolic Use of Space

Presenting a group of words as a title indicates their purpose. Putting quotation marks around them would be redundant!

▶ **Don't place quotation marks around words or phrases for emphasis or to make them more dramatic.**

Examples:

- My new coat came from "Paris."
- Her violin was once played by "Stradivarius."
- On "special" today is the rib roast.
- She was a big "success" in the show.

Often, placing words in quotation marks indicates that you are using the words in opposition to the way you are stating them: The speaker's new coat didn't really come from Paris; it's a joke—get it? Yeah, the violin was played by Stradivarius; we all know it's not true. The rib roast is actually quite expensive. Well, maybe her mother thought she was a great success in the show.

There is a difference between using quotation marks for supposed emphasis and drama, (which is a sign of an amateur writer), and using the marks for ironic distance. For example, take this sentence: He told me that I was not "politically correct" in my language. The term "politically correct" is a trendy term, often overused. The writer who puts quotation marks around it is indicating the he knows this is a trendy term that is often overused, and he is poking a little fun at himself for using it once again.

You cannot say this about the person who writes that her coat came from "Paris." Paris is not a term (it's a city), it is not trendy (it's been with us for centuries). There is no irony here; on the contrary, the reader senses a need to impress.

Too often you see this use of quotation marks on flyers on bulletin boards. "Piano for Sale!" the flyer may say. There is nothing ironic about this piano (unless it's not a piano but a bicycle they are calling a piano), and there is nothing ironic about this sale (unless it's not a sale). This is simply a flyer written by a not-too-bright person who does not know how to punctuate—or write a literate flyer.

▶ **Don't place quotation marks around slang or colloquial expressions except in dialogue.**

Examples:
- She's a "computer nerd."
- He's "nuts."
- They looked "tacky."

Unless there are ironic reasons for writing this way, the writer simply shows himself as amateur.

▶ **Don't use quotation marks around indirect quotations.**

Examples:

- My father said he definitely did not want me to go and that I must listen to him.

You are not directly quoting your father but simply relaying what he said. Quotation marks are not needed.

- He asked Maria whether she knew when she was coming back from her trip to Rome.

This is simply a report of what Maria was asked.

5.8 Punctuation With Quotation Marks

▶ **Periods and commas should go *inside* quotation marks.**

Examples:

- In the newspaper, she was reading an article called "What Students Need to Know."

- In "What Students Need to Know," she read something she and her friends had just discussed.

▶ **Question marks and exclamation points should go *inside* quotation marks if they are a part of the quotation.**

Examples:

- The article was titled "Do the Students Need to Know This?"

- "Stop!" I screamed. "A car is coming!"

- The children in the back seat whined, "Are we there yet?"

▶ **Colons, semicolons, and citation material go *outside* closing quotation marks.**

Examples:

- Cynthia had one thought after seeing "The Stalker": lock the house!

- In *Le Morte d'Arthur,* Malory tells us that objects used in the ceremony of excommunication are "bell, book, and candle"; these phrases are used to signify the power of the Church, or to ridicule its rituals.

▶ **Question marks and exclamation points should go *outside* if they are not part of the quotation.**

Examples:

- I asked her, "Have you read the article, 'What Students Need to Know'?"

- Did you read that short story, "Wait for Me a Little"?

- I'm just crazy about the Marx Brothers in "A Day at the Opera"!

5.9 Single Quotation Marks

Use single quotation marks around a title that is within another quotation.

Examples:

- Caroline said, "I really enjoyed reading 'The Raven,' by Edgar Allan Poe."

- Robert asked, "Do you know what '*Et tu, Brute?*' means, Paul?"

- Paul answered, "Sure. It means 'And you, Brutus?' These were Julius Caesar's dying words to his friend Brutus, who had just stabbed him. They are often translated, 'You too, Brutus?' which is not a literal translation."

5.10 Exercises

Punctuate and add quotation marks where needed. (Some additional space is provided on page 116.)

1. In the stage play Julius Caesar Mark Antony says in his funeral oration for Caesar's corpse Evil that men do lives after them the good is oft interred with their bones.

2. Horatio Hamlet's best friend bid farewell to the dying Hamlet in these words Good Night Sweet Prince.

3. The Grapes of Wrath a novel by John Steinbeck depicts the suffering of American farmworkers in the Depression of the 1930s.

4. Steinbeck took his title from the Book of Revelation in the Bible in which St. John the Divine hears an angel announce that the wicked shall drink wine pressed from the grapes of God's anger.

5. In Othello Shakespeare referring to jealousy calls it a green-eyed monster.

6. Mrs. Malaprop a character in an 18th century play called The Rivals by Richard Sheridan was known for misuing words from her we get the word malapropism which in French means out of place

7. Jonathan Swift coined the term hand-in-glove to describe two people who fit together as precisely as a glove fits a hand.

8. Joseph Conrad's novel Heart of Darkness describes a man's journey into the interior of Africa.

9. The sentry asks Who goes there in some of Shakespeare's plays.

10. I don't care whether this film is politically correct or not I am going to see it

11. My dictionary has 100 pages of A words for example aeroembolism and aminotriazole however it has only one and one-half pages of X words for example xiphosuran and xrophthalmaia.

12. She is a pedicurist but her official title is nail technician.

13. Please read the following books The Practical Stylist Working with Words and Word Mysteries and Histories and also these magazines U.S. News and World Report and Time

14. The magazine House Beautiful carried an article called Where the Water Is

15. Here are three lines of poetry from Shakespeare's *The Tempest.* Write them as if you were incorporating them within the text of a term paper in school.

> Full fathom five my father lies:
>
> Of his bones are coral made;
>
> Those pearls that were his eyes:

_____

_____

_____

_____

_____

16. Write and punctuate the following as if you were quoting it as a passage in a term paper in school:

In their little book The Elements of Style the authors write this paragraph: Hopefully. This once-useful adverb meaning "with hope" has been distorted and is now widely used to mean "I hope" or "it is to be hoped" Such use is not merely wrong it is silly. To say, Hopefully I'll leave on the noon plane is to talk nonsense Do you mean you'll leave on the noon plane in a hopeful frame of mind? Or do you mean you hope you'll leave on the noon plane? Whichever you mean you haven't said it clearly

17. Here are six lines of poetry from "Annabel Lee," by Edgar Allan Poe. Write them below as if you were incorporating them in a term paper in school.

> It was many and many a year ago,
> In a kingdom by the sea,
> That a maiden there lived whom you may know
> By the name of Annabel Lee.
> And this maiden she lived with no other thought
> Than to love and be loved by me.

_____

_____

_____

_____

_____

_____

_____

_____

_____

_____

18. Punctuate the following and put it in proper quotation marks:

In Charles Dickens novel Hard Times a stuffy teacher Mr. Gradgrind has a student define a horse which the student does in forty words and readers still don't know what a horse is.

19. Write this as if you were writing it in the text of a school paper.

> In Stopping by Woods on a Snowy Evening
> Robert Frost closes with
> And miles to go before I sleep,
> And miles to go before I sleep.

_____

_____

_____

_____

_____

_____

_____

20. The children playing with a jumping rope screamed Jump jump jump

21. One student thought the film The Horse Whisperer was what he called really beautiful and another called it silly and corny.

22. Our professor Mr Olsen said You will enjoy reading Walt Whitmans Song of Myself

23. Our professor Mr Olsen asked us Did you enjoy reading Walt Whitmans Song of Myself

24. Jonathan said I am going to Paris but I asked Peter to come with me and he said I wish I could but I have to work over the summer

25. Write one sentence, incorporating all the information, and punctuate it correctly.

In Ars Poetica the poet Archibald MacLeish says
A poem should not mean
But be.

_____

_____

_____

_____

_____

_____

Answers:

_____

_____

_____

_____

_____

_____

_____

_____

5.11 Key to Exercises

1. In the stage play, "Julius Caesar," Mark Antony says in his funeral oration for Caesar's corpse, "Evil that men do lives after them; the good is oft interred with their bones."

2. Horatio, Hamlet's best friend, bid farewell to the dying Hamlet in these words, "Good Night, Sweet Prince."

3. *The Grapes of Wrath*, a novel by John Steinbeck, depicts the suffering of American farmworkers in the Depression of the *1930*'s. (Or you may write *1930*s.)

4. Steinbeck took his title from "The Book of Revelation" in the Bible, in which St. John the Divine hears an angel announce that the wicked shall drink wine pressed from the grapes of God's anger.

5. In "Othello," Shakespeare, referring to jealousy, calls it a "green-eyed monster."

6. Mrs. Malaprop, a character in an 18th century play called "The Rivals," by Richard Sheridan, was known for misusing words; from her we get the word "malapropism," which in French means "out of place."

7. Jonathan Swift coined the term "hand-in-glove" to describe two people who fit together as precisely as a glove fits a hand.

8. Joseph Conrad's novel, *Heart of Darkness*, describes a man's journey into the interior of Africa.

9. The sentry asks, "Who goes there?" in some of Shakespeare's plays.

10. I don't care whether this film is "politically correct" or not, I am going to see it.

11. My dictionary has one-hundred pages of "A" words, for example, "aeroembolism" and "aminotriazole"; however, it has only one and one-half pages of "X" words, for example, "xiphosuran" and "xrophthalmaia."

12. She is a pedicurist, but her official title is "nail technician."

13. Please read the following books, *The Practical Stylist*, *Working with Words,* and *Word Mysteries and Histories*, and these magazines, *U.S. News and World Report*, and *Time*.

14. The magazine, *House Beautiful,* carried an article called "Where the Water Is."

15. In Shakespeare's *Tempest,* he writes, "Full fathom five my father lies: / Of his bones are coral made; / Those pearl that were his eyes:"

    Remember the spaces and slashes designate lines of poetry. Also, remember that you leave off the article when the name of the work follows the author's name.

16. In their little book, *The Elements of Style,* the authors write this paragraph:

    'Hopefully.' This once-useful adverb meaning 'with hope' has been distorted and is now widely used to mean 'I hope,' or 'it is to be hoped.' Such use is not merely wrong, it is silly. To say, 'Hopefully, I'll leave on the noon plane,' is to talk nonsense. Do you mean you'll leave on the noon plane in a hopeful frame of mind? Or do you mean you hope you'll leave on the noon plane? Whichever you mean, you haven't said it clearly.

17. Edgar Allan Poe writes in "Annabel Lee":

    It was many and many years ago,
    In a kingdom by the sea,
    That a maiden there lived whom you may know
    By the name of Annabel Lee.
    And this maiden she lived with no other thought
    Than to love and be loved by me.

Remember that when quoting more than three lines, you write them as in a block quotation.

18. In Charles Dickens' novel, *Hard Times,* a stuffy teacher, Mr. Gradgrind, has a student define a horse, which the student does in forty words, and readers still don't know what a horse is.

19. In "Stopping by Woods on a Snowy Evening," Robert Frost closes with "And miles to go before I sleep, / And miles to go before I sleep."

20. The children playing with a jumping rope screamed, "Jump, jump, jump!"

    Which children? The ones playing with the jumping rope; this is necessary to the sentence, so do not use commas. And notice that the exclamation is within the quotation marks, since they were screaming.

21. One student thought the film, "The Horse Whisperer," was what he called "really beautiful," and another called it "silly and corny."

22. Our professor, Mr. Olsen, said, "You will enjoy reading Walt Whitman's "Song of Myself."

    If this had been written "Professor Olsen," Professor would be considered a title requiring no comma. Here Mr. Olsen is an appositive. The period belongs inside the quotation marks, as usual.

23. Our professor, Mr. Olsen, asked us, "Did you enjoy reading Walt Whitman's "Song of Myself"?

    The question mark belongs outside the quotation marks, since Mr. Olsen asked, not Walt Whitman. And "professor" is not used as a title here, "Mr." is.

24. Jonathan said, "I am going to Paris, but I asked Peter to come with me,' and he said, 'I wish I could, but I have to work over the summer.'"

Notice that a quotation within a quotation is surrounded by single quotation marks. The end carries both the single mark of the inside quotation, and the double marks of the original quotation.

25. In "Ars Poetica," the poet, Archibald MacLeish, says, "A poem should not mean / But be."

Hyphens and Dashes

: — ; / • , ? ! " " ' ( ) - ;

Punctuation adjusts the tone and color and volume till the feeling comes into perfect focus....

—Pico Iyer

6.1 Hyphens

▶ **Use a hyphen to divide a word.**

In the old days of typewriters, this rule was more important than it is now. Our computers do this work for us by spinning the full word to the next line. In either case, a hyphen divides a word at the end of a line, and the word must be divided at a syllable: some-thing, soph-o-more, Ca-ro-li-na, Po-po-ca-te-petl. If you have a need to divide a word today, use your dictionary, which will give you syllable division.

▶ **Use a hyphen to add a prefix to a word.**

Examples:

Pre-World War II	pro-choice	anti-gun
anti-intellectual	all-inclusive	ex-husband
pro-business	co-conspirator	super-mom

▶ **Use a hyphen to add a suffix to a word.**

Examples:

President-elect   president-pro-tem song-fest

▶ **Use a hyphen to divide letter words.**

Examples:

T-shirt	X-ray	L-shaped room
K-rations	U-turn	V-neck

▶ **Use a hyphen in a compound adjective before a noun.**

Hyphens are little creative tools, for they allow you to make up your own words. Someone, at some time, compounded the following adjectives to use before a plain old noun and created new and colorful words.

Examples:

well-earned vacation	blue-green dress
in-house lawyer	light-weight coat
middle-class family	high-heeled shoes
not-too-distant future	fact-finding search
far-reaching legislation	double-barreled shotgun
Western-leaning country	well-tailored suit
hot-dog stand	hot-blooded man
baggage-claim area	medium-security prison
shame-faced smile	sing-song voice
punch-drunk man	sugar-cured ham
first-class cabin	sugar-based drink

❯ Use a hyphen in a compound noun.

Examples:

mother-in-law	fathers-in-law	mid-island
hide-and-seek	go-between	vote-getter
first-class	skin-deep	ship-shape

> **Tip** Some compound nouns were once compound adjectives used before a noun. For example, when you have booked a first-class seat on an airplane, you might say: "I booked first-class." A high-rise building is now often called a high-rise. When hyphen use evolves, it tends to drop the hyphen and close the two words into one solid word.

6.2 Hyphenated Numbers

Use a hyphen to divide numbers between 21 and 99.

Examples:

- The ninety-eight-pound woman carried a twenty-three-pound dog.

- She is sixty-eight and will be sixty-nine in February.

- The hog weighs eighty-two pounds, twenty-two pounds more than the sixty-pound pig.

- There are fifty-four students in the dancing class, thirty-seven in choir, and twenty-three in drama.

- The glass is two-thirds full. The bottle is three-fourths empty.

- It took me a week and one-half to get an appointment with the dentist.

We will look at how to write numbers in other contexts in Chapter 8.

The Suspended Hyphen

You don't need to know this term so much as you need to know the concept. And the concept is best explained when illustrated.

> The store sold five-, ten-, and fifteen-pound boxes of cookies. It also sold children's-, juniors'-, and women's-size dresses.

You see here that the hyphen is indeed suspended; the reader does not reach the "pound" or the "size" until after the list of adjectives. The two sentences could also be compressed into one: "The store sold cookies in boxes of five, ten, and fifteen pounds, and it sold dresses in sizes for children, juniors, and women." But if the writer has a good reason for suspending the sense of the sentence—or simply chooses to do so for variety—she punctuates it in the way previously illustrated.

 Tip Since the English language continues to evolve, some words once written with a hyphen have now become solid words. For example, *wild-life* is now written *wildlife*, and *bell-boy* is now written *bellboy*. For that matter, *semi-colon* is now written *semicolon*. Two words often become a hyphenated word, then later become one word.

Technological words, once written with hyphens, have now become one word—*on-line*, for example, is now written *online*. When in doubt, check your dictionary. If you can't find the word there, hyphenate it, until someone tells you differently.

6.3 Exercises

Place hyphens and all other punctuation in the appropriate places.

1. Don't eat that Priscilla who was always watching her weight exclaimed Its sugar based cereal

2. People in most service professions have nine to five jobs therefore they often work in shifts

3. In the old movie that ran between 8 and 10 p m John Wayne wore a ten gallon hat he also wore leather soled boots.

4. The old daisy wheel printer became obsolete so the not for profit office in which Meg was working got a new laser printer.

5. We went to the lake to go fishing but we found that the cabin was bug infested so we came home after a day and one half

6. Herberts mother in law grew up in the mid twentieth century and had a lot of old fashioned ideas

7. He's a first class guy Jerry said of his red headed friend Moe who had changed from his brown and green plaid jacket into a natty white suit

8. Carlos put on his T shirt went to get his chest X rayed then came home to his L shaped room and read his e mail.

9. Sam told his ex wife that he would keep the children over the summer and she gave him a big red lipped smile

10. After a fact finding search the president elect said he would put in far reaching legislation that was pro business.

11. At the wedding Steven wore an expensive light weight tux and Sasha wore an off the shoulder gown with a three foot train on which Molly and Courtney insisted on stepping as they followed her down the flower strewn aisle.

12. After Sasha married she found herself with a mother in law a father in law two step sisters in law and an aunt on Stevens mothers side who spoke very loudly and annoyed everyone

13. The couple booked a first class flight to Hawaii and stayed in a gorgeous high rise apartment with a view of the ocean so Sasha nearly forgot about all the in laws and the annoying aunt

14. Steven thought Sashas bleach blond mother very bossy and her bald headed father quite gruff but he decided to put up with it anyway because he loved Sasha

15. Their new home contained a twenty foot long kitchen a ten foot by twelve foot dining room and three bedrooms that were ten twelve and fourteen feet square.

16. Their neighbors Whitney and Cece took a six mile hike through the woods and returned with wildflowers for the bride and groom.

17. Steven and Sasha were glad they had moved to a cul de sac near a sushi take out on Lennon Ave in Trenton New Jersey and felt in the not too distant future they would learn to love their neighbors and to live happily ever after

18. Meanwhile back in New York City the six foot six inch man on the subway looked down on most people in the car.

19. The taxi cab driver was upset that the man chose to ride the over crowded subway instead of hiring a cab in which case the cabby might get a three dollar tip

20. Wendy who had just flown into Atlanta told her son David to stand in the baggage claim area and watch for red and black luggage.

21. David stood by a man in a blue green T shirt with a V neck who wanted to talk about the Baltimore Orioles and David a baseball fan was happy to hear it and gave him a snaggle toothed grin.

22. When the brand new luggage came David and his mother carried the two twenty pound suitcases about fifty feet to the exit and waited for David's dad to pick them up in a rental car.

23. I'm hungry said David as they passed a hot dog stand so his dad stopped the car and paid two dollars each for the hot dogs and one dollar and fifty cents each for the soft drinks.

24. Wendy wanted nothing from the roadside stand all she wanted was to lie in the back seat of the car and enjoy her well earned vacation she hoped it would start soon

25. When the vacation was over the family took a business class flight back to Houston and all agreed they had had a super terrific trip to Atlanta and Wendy looked forward to a visit from her step sisters Robbyn and Jill

6.4 Key to Exercises

1. "Don't eat that!" Priscilla, who was always watching her weight, exclaimed. "It's sugar-based cereal."

2. People in most service professions have nine-to-five jobs; therefore, they often work in shifts.

3. In the old movie that ran between 8 and 10 p.m., John Wayne wore a ten-gallon hat; he also wore leather-soled boots.

4. The old daisy-wheel printer became obsolete, so the not-for-profit office in which Meg was working got a new laser printer.

5. We went to the lake to go fishing, but we found that the cabin was bug-infested, so we came home after a day and one-half.

   In conversation, you may say "a day and a half," but use the formal "one-half" in writing.

6. Herbert's mother-in-law grew up in the mid-twentieth century and had a lot of old-fashioned ideas.

7. "He's a first-class guy," Jerry said of his red-headed friend Moe, who had changed from his brown-and-green-plaid jacket into a natty white suit.

8. Carlos put on his T-shirt, went to get his chest X-rayed, then came home to his L-shaped room and read his e-mail.

9. Sam told his ex-wife that he would keep the children over the summer, and she gave him a big red-lipped smile.

10. After a fact-finding search, the President-elect said he would put in far-reaching legislation that was pro-business.

    If this sentence refers to the President of the U.S., then the capitalization above is correct.

11. At the wedding, Steven wore an expensive, light-weight tux, and Sasha wore an off-the-shoulder gown with a three-foot train on which Molly and Courtney insisted on stepping, as they followed her down the flower-strewn aisle.

12. After Sasha married, she found herself with a mother-in-law, a father-in-law, two step-sisters-in-law, and an aunt on Steven's mother's side, who spoke very loudly and annoyed everyone.

    Notice that the correct term is "sisters-in-law" not "sister-in-laws."

13. The couple booked a first-class flight to Hawaii and stayed in a gorgeous high-rise apartment with a view of the ocean, so Sasha nearly forgot about all the in-laws and the annoying aunt.

14. Steven thought Sasha's bleach-blond mother very bossy, and her bald-headed father quite gruff, but he decided to put up with it anyway, because he loved Sasha.

15. Their new home contained a twenty-foot-long kitchen, a ten-foot-by-twelve-foot dining room, and three bedrooms that were ten-, twelve-, and fourteen-feet square.

    Notice all the compound adjectives that require hyphens, and notice the suspended adjectives here.

16. Their neighbors, Whitney and Cece, took a six-mile hike through the woods and returned with wildflowers for the bride and groom.

Flowers are not generally capitalized, unless they indicate a proper name like Windsor Rose.

17. Steven and Sasha were glad they had moved to a cul-de-sac near a sushi take-out on Lennon Ave. in Trenton, New Jersey and felt in the not-too-distant future they would learn to love their neighbors and to live happily ever after.

Notice there is no comma after New Jersey. Why? Recall the comma rule in complex sentences. If the last part of this sentence read "and *they* felt in the not-too-distant-future," *etc.*, the sentence would become compound and would require the comma.

18. Meanwhile, back in New York City, the six-foot-six-inch man on the subway looked down on most people in the car.

19. The taxi-cab driver was upset that the man chose to ride the over-crowded subway instead of hiring a cab, in which case the cabby might get a three-dollar tip.

"Taxi-cab" is hyphenated here, because it is a compound adjective describing "driver," but you could just as well write "taxicab," since this word is evolving into one solid word.

20. Wendy, who had just flown into Atlanta, told her son, David, to stand in the baggage-claim area and watch for their red-and-black luggage.

21. David stood by a man in a blue-green T-shirt with a V-neck, who wanted to talk about the Baltimore Orioles, and David, a baseball fan, was happy to hear it and gave him a snaggle-toothed grin.

22. When the luggage came, David and his mother carried the two twenty-pound suitcases about fifty feet to the exit and waited for David's dad to pick them up in a rental car.

23. "I'm hungry," said David, as they passed a hot-dog stand, so his dad stopped the car and paid two dollars each for the hot dogs and one dollar and fifty cents each for the soft drinks.

24. Wendy wanted nothing from the roadside stand; all she wanted was to lie in the back seat of the car and enjoy her well-earned vacation; she hoped it would start soon.

    This group of words contains three independent clauses. To avoid writing a *run-on* sentence, you must break them up with semicolons or periods. Either is fine.

25. When the vacation was over, the family took a business-class flight back to Houston, and all agreed they had had a super-terrific trip to Atlanta and looked forward to a visit from Wendy's step-sisters, Robbyn and Jill.

    You probably wouldn't be wrong if you wrote *stepsisters*. This is another of those words making its way into the language without its hyphen. Good news: hot dog is not yet written hotdog! But who knows when?

6.5 Dashes

Dashes (—) are small nuances of punctuation. They indicate slight or delicate variations in tone, color, or meaning in a sentence. They can also be used to create drama.

▶ **Use dashes to add explanatory material to a statement.**

Example:

- He asked Alice—the girl who sat next to him in biology class—to the senior prom.

- With his duffel bag—a new one purchased at the store around the corner—Patrick headed for the airport.

- It took him an hour to get ready—to get out of bed, find his clothes, take a shower, eat his breakfast—before he caught the 8 o'clock train.

- The notion that this woman was his mother—the woman who had given him life and raised him to manhood—was never lost on the son who adored her.

- It was dark outside, but she could still see the spring flowers—tulips and daffodils—blooming in the garden.

▶ **Use dashes within a sentence to add emphasis.**

Example:

> I was tired—sick and tired—of revising papers for my writing class.

▶ **Use a dash to add a tag word or line to a sentence.**

Examples:

- I want a double banana split with butterscotch and chocolate sauce—and don't forget the cherry!

- She had forgotten to pack her most valuable item—her hair dryer.

▶ **Use dashes to indicate a long pause or to slow down a sentence.**

Examples:

- First, I need to call my dad, and then—well—I guess I should call my grandfather and invite him, too.

- "What—what do you mean?" he asked, startled at her question.

Dash indicates hesitation in speech.

▶ **Use a dash to indicate a change of tone or direction in a sentence.**

Example:

> I enjoy the company of my younger sister—but I don't want her around all the time.

Notice that in all previous cases where a sentence is interrupted in the middle with dashes, the part of the sentence after the final dash goes on to complete the first thought—as if the dashes had not interrupted.

More Examples of the Use of the Dash

Sometimes dashes can be used to do several things at once.

Example:

- He was afraid she would get angry with him, shout at him in public—in short, make a scene.

This dash is used to add a tag line, add emphasis, and show hesitation or break in thought.

- He picked up the heavy suitcase and asked, "What's in this—concrete?"

The dash indicates hesitation and tag word.

 Tip) With some computer software, dashes are made by using two hyphens together (--) with no space before, between, or after. Other software makes a solid dash. Still other software will automatically convert two hyphens to a solid dash.

Do not use one hyphen (-) as a dash. Use two hyphens (--) instead. This is a good rule—and don't forget it!

6.6 Exercises

After the sentences, write the reason—or reasons—the dash is being used.

1. By the time the film was over—and this was the most important thing about it—Jeffrey had realized that it was not about the superficial story, but about technology encroaching on our lives.

   _____

2. "So," he said accusingly, "this is your bottom line—money."

   _____

3. "Well," he began, before she jumped in, "are you satisfied now—?"

   _____

4. It was hot—really hot—but we hit the city streets to find jobs.

   _____

5. Well, you know Dad; he sits in that chair every day—doesn't even rock—until it's time for the news.

   _____

6. I said, "Really—really, John—you should know better than that!"

   _____

7. Her voice on the phone—"Uh-huh, uh-huh, sure, sure, oh I see"—let us know there was trouble between them.

   _____

8. "Listen, Dad, I was going to clean up the yard, but—well, you know how it is—Steve called with tickets to the ballgame."

9. Martha said, "Mmm, brownies!"—as she reached for one from the plate.

10. "No, well, see"—Carl grabbed his coat—"we'll just be gone a little while."

11. "What? You're broke?" he interjected. "I guess you"—he put his hand in his pocket—"I guess you need a loan, then."

12. "I didn't—uh—sleep very well last night," he explained.

13. The plot of the film was trite—love affairs, car crashes, lovers' quarrels, car crashes—it was a truly dumb movie.

14. He looked at the books on his shelf—some new, some tattered, some without dust jackets—and wondered whether he'd ever get around to reading them all.

15. What do you want for dinner—salmon, steak, sushi, or surf and turf?

16. "Where do you think I—?"

17. The costs—food and housing—were increasing every day.

18. The operator said, "Please deposit—an—additional—fifty cents—now."

19. "Okay, then—" he agreed. "If that's what you want to do. But listen—"

20. Melanie—no matter how stubborn and pig-headed she was, and no matter how lazy she could be sometimes, and no matter that she borrowed my sweater and stained it—was my sister.

21. It was a heartbreaking—and finally, just a wrenching—story.

22. His family and mine were—and still are—close.

23. She dropped out of school to—what else?—get married.

24. He is creating an international Book Town in that little village—stocking the place with one million books.

25. The new mayor will face many problems—declining revenue, poor schools, increased taxes, aging population—during her first year in office.

6.7 Key to Exercises

1. By the time the film was over—and this was the most important thing about it—Jeffrey had realized that it was not about the superficial story, but about technology encroaching on our lives.

    Material enclosed in dashes adds new information and emphasis.

2. "So," he said, accusingly, "this is your bottom line— money."

    The pause, indicated by the dash, adds emphasis and strengthens the importance of the tag word.

3. "Well," he began, before she jumped in, "are you satisfied now—?"

    Dash shows hesitation, interruption of thought, unfinished comment.

4. It was hot—really hot—but we hit the city streets to find jobs.

    Material within dashes adds emphasis.

5. Well, you know Dad; he sits in that chair every day—and doesn't even rock—until it's time for the news.

    Material within dashes adds further information.

6. I said, "Really—really, John—you should know better than that!"

    Words within dashes add emphasis.

7. Her voice on the phone—"Uh-huh, uh, huh, sure, sure, oh I see"—let us know there was trouble between them.
   Material within dashes shows hesitation and adds information.

8. Listen, Dad, I was going to clean up the yard, but—well, you know how it is—Steven called with tickets to the ballgame.
   Material within dashes adds hesitation, a little emphasis, as speaker tries to think of his reply.

9. Martha said, "Mmm, brownies!"—as she reached for one from the plate.
   Material after dash adds emphasis to the tag line.

10. "No, well, see"—Carl grabbed his coat—"we'll just be gone a little while."
    Material within dashes adds information, detail.

11. "What? You're broke?" he interjected. "I guess you"—he put his hand in his pocket—"I guess you need a loan, then."
    Material within dashes adds detail, information, color.

12. "I didn't—uh—sleep very well last night," he explained.
    Material within dashes shows hesitation.

13. The plot of the film was trite—love affairs, car crashes, lovers' quarrels, car crashes—it was a truly dumb movie.
    Material within dashes offers new information and detail.

14. He looked at the books on his shelf—some new, some tattered, some without dust jackets—and wondered whether he'd ever get around to reading them all.
    Material within dashes gives information and detail.

15. What do you want for dinner—salmon, steak, sushi, or surf and turf?

    Material after dash adds a tag line and gives new information.

16. "Where do you think I—?"

    Dash indicates voice hesitation, thought interruption.

17. The costs—food and housing—were increasing every day.

    New information, detail, emphasis indicated within dashes.

18. The operator said, "Please deposit—an—additional—fifty cents—now."

    Dashes indicate hesitation, used for clarity and emphasis.

19. "Okay, then—" he agreed. "If that's what you want to do. But listen—"

    Dashes indicate hesitation, perhaps interruption at the end of the remark.

20. Melanie—no matter how stubborn and pig-headed she was, and no matter how lazy she could be sometimes, and no matter that she borrowed my sweater and stained it—was my sister.

    Material within dashes adds information, detail, color, emphasis, delays the punch line for humorous effect.

21. It was a heartbreaking—and finally, just a wrenching—story.

    Material within dashes adds emphasis, information.

22. His family and mine were—and still are—close.

    Material within dashes adds information and emphasis.

23. She dropped out of school to—what else?—get married.

    Material within dashes adds emphasis.

24. He is creating an international Book Town in that little village—stocking the place with one million books.

    Material after dash adds information, emphasis, tag line.

25. The new mayor will face many problems—declining revenue, poor schools, increased taxes, aging population—during her first year in office.

    Material within dashes adds new information, detail.

Capitalization

: — ; / • , ? ! " " ' ( ) - ;

A rebellion was surely marked when
e. e. cummings first felt free to commit 'God' to
the lower case.

—Pico Iyer

7.1 First Words

▶ **Capitalize the first word of a sentence.**

Examples:

- She is writing a sentence.
- She will always capitalize the first word.
- He will write correctly.

▶ **When you are using a quotation in a paper, capitalize the first word of the quotation.**

Hamlet said, "To be or not to be."

But if you are quoting indirectly, introducing the quotation with the word "that," do not capitalize the first letter of the quotation.

Example:

> He said that "to be or not to be" was a quotation from "Hamlet."

▶ **Following a colon, capitalize the first letter when it precedes a complete sentence.**

Example:

> The letter continued with these words: "Please call me as soon as possible."

▶ **If the words following a colon do *not* form a sentence,** do not **capitalize the first word.**

Example:

> This is what he saw from his window: houses, trees, yards, and cars.

▶ **When quoting poems, follow the capitalization of the poet precisely.**

Example:

> A Book of Verses underneath the Bough,
>
> A Jug of Wine, a Loaf of Bread—and Thou
>
> > —Omar Khayyam, "The Rubaiyat"

7.2 Proper Names and Titles

Proper names, government bodies and monuments, historical eras, religions, religious figures, ethnic groups, countries, institutions, corporations, trade names, streets, and roads are capitalized.

Examples:

William Shakespeare	Captain John Smith
Elvis Presley	Mary Shelley
The United States	Europe
Great Britain	The White House
Congress	Library of Congress
Lincoln Memorial	The Middle Ages
God	Buddha
Catholics	Methodists
Columbia University	New York University
Hewlett Packard	Word Perfect
Prospect Road	South Center Street
The Lonesome Dove Inn	The Hilton Hotel

 Tip Proper nouns name specific persons, places, and things. All the other nouns are common nouns—man, woman, child, baby, singer, expert, bread, town, fish, toenails —and are not capitalized.

▶ **Capitalize titles.**

Examples:

President Bush	Justice Ruth Bader Ginsburg
Former President Clinton	Justice William O. Douglas
Professor Jonathan Martin	Dr. Thomas Franklin

 Tip Do not capitalize the word "president" when it does not precede a proper name, unless you are talking about the President of the United States. Example: George W. Bush is President. Charles Baker is president of the Rotary Club.

▶ **Capitalize Mother, Father, Aunt, Uncle and other family relationship words only if they are part of a name, or if they are used to substitute for a name.**

Examples:

> Mother Theresa, Aunt Mary, Uncle Hank, Brother John, Mother and Father (or Mom and Dad) celebrated the holiday.

 Tip) Do not capitalize *my mother* and *my father* or *his mom and dad*. Why? The words—my mom, my dad, my sister—do not stand for a name. The word is treated as a possessive.

7.3 Adjectives Formed by Proper Nouns

Capitalize adjectives formed by proper nouns.

Examples:

African American expert	Catholic wedding
Hispanic writer	Italian filmmaker
British journalist	German car
American hamburger	Cuban cigar

7.4 Geographic Regions

Capitalize geographic regions.

Examples:

North	South	East
West	Midwest	Southeast

Tip Though you capitalize geographic regions (the North, the South), you do not capitalize these words when you are speaking of directions.

Example:

Turn south on Main Street. He lives west of I-75. We took the north fork of the road and turned east at the mall.

Do *not* capitalize seasons (spring, fall, winter) unless these are connected to an event: Spring Festival, Fall Book Fair, Winter Ball.

7.5 Exercises

Correctly punctuate the sentences and indicate appropriate capitalization.

1. vanity fair is the title of a novel written by william makepeace thackery in 1848 who took the title from john bunyan's religious allegory the pilgrim's progress, written in 1678.

2. in his novel bunyan wrote about a little town called vanity in which tempting wares and worldly pleasures were offered for sale at a fair by devils and other questionable persons

3. african american playwright lorraine hansberry wrote a drama for the stage called a raisin in the sun her title paraphrases a poem by langston hughes in which he wrote "a dream deferred dries up like a raisin in the wind "

4. american dramatist marc connelly wrote a play called green pastures the title of which he took from psalm 23 in which these words occur he helps me to lie down in green pastures.

5. ben ames williams wrote a novel in the 1940s called leave her to heaven he took the title from words spoken to hamlet by the ghost of hamlets father.

6. shakespeare of course wrote hamlet and the "her" in his use of leave her to heaven referred to hamlet s mother queen Gertrude who married her brother-in-law murderer of hamlets father

7. william goldings popular novel lord of the flies took its name from the bible Kings II 1 in which the lord of the flies is another name for satan or a false god

8. in t s eliots poem the hollow men eliot uses the expression Mr Kurtz, he dead, speaking of a character he took from joseph conrads heart of darkness.

9. novelist ernest hemingway borrowed the title of his famous 1926 book the sun also rises from the biblical passage ecclesiastes l 5

10. in ode to a nightingale poet john keats used the words tender is the night later f scott fitzgerald chose those words for the title of his 1934 novel about a mentally ill woman

11. in 1929 american writer william faulkner wrote a novel the sound and the fury the title of which he took from william shakespeares macbeth

12. in the 15th century a fanatic dominican friar named savonarola confiscated books paintings mirrors lip rouges and other items of "vanity" and burned them in a raging fire in a piazza in florence italy

13. savonarolas fire in the piazza in florence was the inspiration for the title of 20th century author tom wolfes satirical book the bonfire of the vanities.

14. one year our class took a trip to washington d c and visited the white house and many government buildings including the congress and the senate and saw the washington monument and the lincoln memorial.

15. we visited the white house and the capitol but we did not see president bush

16. robert woodward and carl bernstein gained fame for their exposé of the nixon white house in their book all the presidents men.

17. it may startle some people to learn that the autobiography of malcolm x was not written by malcolm x but by alex haley.

18. in the late 60s joan didion wrote an essay called slouching to bethlehem before that william butler yeats had used those words in his poem the second coming taking them from st john the divine in the book of revelation in the bible

19. winston churchill who began his writing career as a correspondent in the boer war wrote a six volume history of world war II.

20. in the early 1970s dee brown described the white mans conquest of america from the point of view of the native american in bury my heart at wounded knee

21. adolf hitlers book mein kampf which he wrote in 1923 while imprisoned for attempting to overthrow the german government is translated into english as my struggle

22. german religious leader martin luther 1485-1546 became the leader of the protestant reformation when he posted his ninety-five theses on the church door

23. last winter emily and her son took a trip to the south where they stayed until after christmas day

24. englishman john stuart mill 1806-1873 wrote a political tract *On Liberty* which takes the position that the state may interfere with the freedom of the individual only to protect other individuals

25. american poet robert frost wrote the following little poem called the span of life

> The old dog barks backward without getting up,
> I can remember when he was a pup.

_____

_____

_____

_____

_____

7.6 Key to Exercises

1. *Vanity Fair* is the title of a novel written by William Makepeace Thackery in 1848, who took the title from John Bunyan's religious allegory, *The Pilgrim's Progress,* written in 1678.

2. In his novel, Bunyan wrote about a little town called Vanity, in which tempting wares and worldly pleasures were offered for sale at a fair by devils and other questionable persons.

3. African American playwright, Lorraine Hansberry, wrote a drama for the stage called *A Raisin in the Sun.* Her title paraphrases a poem by Langston Hughes in which he wrote: "A dream deferred dries up like a raisin in the wind."

4. American dramatist, Marc Connelly, wrote a play called "Green Pastures," the title of which he took from Psalm 23 in which these words occur: "He helps me to lie down in green pastures."

5. Ben Ames Williams wrote a novel in the 1940s called "Leave Her to Heaven." He took the title from words spoken to Hamlet by the ghost of Hamlet's father.

6. Shakespeare, of course, wrote "Hamlet," and the "her" in his use of "Leave her to Heaven" referred to Hamlet's mother, Queen Gertrude, who married her brother-in-law, murderer of Hamlet's father.

7. William Golding's popular novel, "Lord of the Flies," took its name from the Bible, II Kings, in which the Lord of the Flies is another name for Satan or a false god.

8. In T. S. Eliot's poem, "The Hollow Men," Eliot uses the expression, "Mr. Kurtz, he dead," speaking of a character he took from Joseph Conrad's "Heart of Darkness."

9. Novelist Ernest Hemingway borrowed the title of his famous 1926 book, *The Sun Also Rises,* from the biblical passage, Ecclesiastes 1:5.

10. In "Ode to a Nightingale," poet John Keats used the words, "tender is the night." Later, F. Scott Fitzgerald chose those words for the title of his 1934 novel about a mentally ill woman.

11. In 1929, American writer William Faulkner wrote a novel, *The Sound and the Fury,* the title of which he took from William Shakespeare's "Macbeth."

12. In the 15th century, a fanatic Dominican friar named Savonarola confiscated books, paintings, mirrors, lip rouges, and other items of "vanity" and burned them in a raging fire in a piazza in Florence, Italy.

13. Savonarola's fire in the piazza was the inspiration for the title of 20th century author Tom Wolfe's satirical book, *The Bonfire of the Vanities.*

14. One year, our class took a trip to Washington, D.C. and visited the White House and many government buildings, including the Congress and the Senate and saw the Washington Monument and the Lincoln Memorial.

15. We visited the White House and the Capitol, but we did not see President Bush.

16. Robert Woodward and Carl Bernstein gained fame for their exposé of the Nixon White House in their book *All the President's Men.*

17. It may startle some people to learn that *The Autobiography of Malcolm X* was not written by Malcolm X, but by Alex Haley.

18. In the late *60*'s, Joan Didion wrote an essay called "Slouching to Bethlehem." Before that, William Butler Yeats had used those words in his poem, "The Second Coming," taking them from St. John the Divine in the Book of Revelation in the Bible.

19. Winston Churchill, who began his writing career as a correspondent in the Boer War, wrote a six-volume history of World War II.

20. In the early 1970's, Dee Brown described the white man's conquest of America from the point of view of the Native American in *Bury My Heart at Wounded Knee.*

21. Adolf Hitler's book, *Mein Kampf,* which he wrote in 1923 while imprisoned for attempting to overthrow the German government, is translated into English as *My Struggle.*

22. German religious leader Martin Luther (1485-1546) became the leader of the Protestant Reformation, when he posted his "Ninety-Five Theses" on the church door.

    Note that the range of numbers in parenthesis denotes the years Martin Luther lived.

23. Last winter Emily and her son took a trip to the South, where they stayed until after Christmas Day.

24. Englishman John Stuart Mill (1806-1873) wrote a political tract, *On Liberty*, which takes the position that the state may interfere with the freedom of the individual only to protect other individuals.

25. American poet Robert Frost wrote the following little poem called "The Span of Life": "The old dog barks backward without getting up, / I can remember when he was a pup."

Abbreviations, Numbers, and Italics

: — ; / • , ? ! "" ' () - ;

8

Punctuation, in fact, is a labor of love.

—Pico Iyer

Abbreviations and numbers are handled differently in different contexts. In magazine and newspaper writing, for example, where every space and line count, articles must be written very tightly. Since space is money, words are money. In these cases, more words are abbreviated and more numbers written as numerals than happens in academic writing. Editors of journalistic pieces know the style used there, and if that is your ambition or intent, you will need to find a *New York Times* stylebook, or another, to help you. When writing for high school, college, or university courses, you can feel comfortable using the guidelines in *Better Punctuation.* Be sure **always** to ask your teachers or professors what guidelines they prefer and follow those.

8.1 Proper Names

Abbreviate titles following or preceding proper names, no matter what kind of paper or publication you are writing for.

Examples:

Mrs. Mary Webster	Mr. Bert Bernstein
Dr. Amos Hartung	Prof. Marcus Tweed
Gen. Colin Powell	Col. Warren Blackburn
Rev. Joseph Murray	Cynthia Wald, J.D.
Samuel G. King, LL.B.	Mr. Gary Webster Jr.

Mr. Gary Webster Jr. is written without a comma before "Jr."

When addressing physicians or professors, you should write Amos Hartung, M.D., or Marcus Tweed, Ph.D.

 Tip It is not good form to write Dr. Amos Hartung, M.D. or Dr. Marcus Tweed, Ph.D. Use one title or the other, but not both.

▶ **Abbreviate company names when you are addressing envelopes, inside addresses, and doing official business.**

Examples:

- General Motors Corp.
- Maxwell and Taylor & Co.
- Cypress Research, Inc.

 Tip Corp. and Co. are not preceded by a comma; Inc. *is* preceded by a comma.

However, if you are using these terms in text (and not as part og the company name), spell them out. For example:

Sears, Roebuck & Co. has a company catalogue as well as retail stores.

8.2 Numbers

▶ **In writing academic papers, spell out units of measurement.**

Examples:

- Please indent ten inches for a quotation.
- The book costs twenty dollars.
- Mark Twain had an office fifteen feet square.
- Twenty-two percent of those surveyed returned the survey.

▶ **In charts and graphs, and when writing scores, statistics, decimals and fractions, and other non-textual communications, use symbols and figures.**

Examples:

- Surveys returned: 22%.
- Please remit $20 for the book.
- Indent here (10"). (" is the symbol for inches)
- Office: 15'x15'. (' is the symbol for feet)
- Average age: 54.
- He owned 66.52% of the stock.
- The driveway was 32 1/2 feet long.
- They set the alarm for 6:45, but did not get up until 7:15.

▶ **When using numbers, if you can write them out in one or two words, do so.**

Examples:

- It was thirty-two years before the woman found her wedding ring, which she had lost in 1960.

- She was twenty-three years old, her mother was forty-seven, her father was fifty, and her younger brother was eighteen. Her great-grandfather was 103.

- The man had twenty-one stitches in his arm.

- The farm was 280 acres and the pond on it was four acres. They bought it for $350,000.00.

- The CD cost $37.50.

 Tip Do not use a numeral to start a sentence. Spell it out, or rewrite the sentence. The following sentences have been rewritten:

> Two-hundred people came to the game.
> *or* The fans numbered 200.

It would be bad form if you started either of the following sentences with the numerals: George Orwell's book was called *1984*. The Civil War began in 1861.

8.3 Italics

Italicize words for four basic reasons: to differentiate long works from short works; to emphasize words; to indicate non-English words, and to write words, letters, or numbers used as terms.

▶ **To differentiate long works from short works**, italicize book titles, such as *War and Peace*. (Put short works, such as poems, in quotation marks: "To His Coy Mistress.") Other italicized works are outlined on pages 157 and 158.

❱ **To emphasize words:**

When I say No, I mean *No.*

❱ **To indicate non-English words:**

A famous quotation of Rene Decartes is *cogito, ergo, sum.* ("I think, therefore, I am.")

❱ **To write words, letters, or numbers used as terms:**

- You misspelled *harassed.*
- The best student in the class made all *A*'s.
- She was born in the *70*s.

Titles of Works

Italicize the title of long works and other items, including these below:

Books:

Lonesome Dove, Truth and Consequences: How Colleges and Universities Meet Public Crises

Films and Videos:

Star Trek, The Princess Bride, Breakfast at Tiffany's

Long Poems:

Song of Myself, Leaves of Grass, Il Penseroso, Hero and Leander

Magazines, Journals, Newspapers:

The New Yorker, Women & the Law, Newsday

Televison Series:

The West Wing, The Capitol Gang, Nightline

Radio Series:

Fresh Air, All Things Considered

Paintings and Sculpture:
Jackson Pollack's *Blue Poles*, Lee Krasner's *Peacock*

Plays:
Annie Get Your Gun, Proof, Copenhagen, Oklahoma! Noises Off, The Iceman Cometh
Though these can also be placed in quotation marks.

CD's:
The Best of Nina Simone, Louis Armstrong: The Hot Fives and Hot Sevens

Websites:
Amazon.com, Google, Alta Vista, Ask Jeeves, Yahoo

Software:
Word Perfect, Microsoft

Musical Works:
Stravinsky's *Le Sacre du Printemps, The Firebird Suite*

Pamphlets or Documents:
The Declaration of Independence, The Constitution of the United States of America

Ships, Aircraft, Trains:
QE II, Arizona, Challenger, Air Force One, Amtrak's *Silver Star*

Non-English words

Examples:

- Flaubert said, *"Le mot juste,"* meaning "the right word."

- She cried *larme de crocodile,* or crocodile tears.

- He wrote *sesquipedalia verba*—in words a foot and one-half long.

- The school's motto was *quaere verum,* or seek the truth.

- She graduated *summa cum laude,* with highest honors.

 Tip Don't italicize anything you have put in quotation marks unless it is a non-English word.
Example:
"Hola," she answered.

For Emphasis

Examples:
- "He said *what?*"
- I told you, I *will not* go.
- *"Could you repeat that?"* she asked, incredulous.
- She read all *fifty-two* of *The Great Books of the Western World?*

Letters, Words, or Numbers Used as Terms

Examples:
- "You did not use *effect* correctly," the teacher said. "You should have used *affect.*"
- The Wildcat team had gold *W*'s on their jackets.
- If you made in the *90*'s on your final exam, I'd say that was pretty good.

8.4 Exercises

Punctuate all the sentences below.

1. When my Italian friend calls me she often says ciao instead of goodbye

2. The guest list consisted of Dr David Waring Ms. Beverly Barton J S Goodwin Jr Marcus Welby M D Mrs Thomas Huntington and Miss Marple

3. He wrote an angry letter about his winter heating bill to Cygnet Oil and The Gastly Corp

4. The weekly comic newspaper in Paris Le Canard Enchaine carried a scathing satire of a local politician

5. In France April Fool's Day is referred to as poisson d'avril

6. Sundance catalogue mailed from Salt Lake City Utah advertises Cocuchas pottery urns made by hand in Mexico "with clay mixed by bare feet from volcanic ash, sand, and water" and fired in charcoal pits

7. 13 people were injured when a bus collided with a truck in Las Vegas according to a newsletter The Last Word published in January 2002

8. In his book The Writer's Way author Jack Rawlins says that the way a baby teaches itself to talk is an excellent way to learn language skills

9. Adam Gopnick in his book Paris to the Moon wrote that the men of the Paris Propre come down his street every night to collect garbage

10. In Woe is I The Grammarphobe's Guide to Better English in Plain English, Patricia T. O'Conner in a section called A Cure for the Whom-Sick writes Now for the good news. In almost all cases you can use who instead of whom in conversation or in informal writing, like personal letters and casual memos

11. In their new 4,000 square foot house they had a 20 foot by 20 foot library and a 10 by 12 foot exercise room

12. In their book, Better Spelling in 30 Minutes a Day, authors Crosby and Emery say as follows Media is a plural form of medium therefore we must say the media are never the media is.

13. The students listed as their favorite foods swiss cheese italian bread boston baked beans and english muffins.

14. Mr Jerome L Tarp Jr is currently working for Pioneer Corp in Dallas and his cousin Martin Tarp took a position with Ashland Food Inc in Boulder Colorado

15. The professor of our class has just come back from teaching at a lycee in France and will return there to direct a program in concentrated Français-Anglais next spring

16. The president traveled on his private plane air force one to germany last week accompanied by his wife and his staff of six

17. The city council is dominated by the democratic party but the county tax commission has a majority of republicans on its roster

18. The books on the shelf in my history professors office include Churchill by Martin Gilbert The Chief The Life of William Randolph Hearst by David Nasaw The Trust by Susan E. Tifft and Alex S. Jones American Caesar by William Manchester Winchell by Neal Gabler and The Power Broker by Robert A. Caro

19. While studying French together Calvin paused and said to Hannah I love you beaucoup which surprised Hannah so much that she replied I love you de plus belle

20. In his book Crazy English Richard Lederer defines oxymoron as a figure of speech in which two incongruous contradictory terms are yoked together in a small space, for example, good grief

21. Lederer who frequently comments on national public radio NPR goes on to say that the word oxymoron is itself oxymoronic because it is formed from two Greek roots of opposite meaning—oxys meaning sharp and keen and moros meaning foolish the same root that gives us the word moron

22. For their study Iron Bronze and Golden Women the researchers surveyed 1,045 women by sending them a 3 page questionnaire and were surprised when 81.2% of the women returned the completed survey document

23. One researcher exclaimed in disbelief This is amazing nobody gets such a high return on surveys her partner was equally startled What? an 80% return? We must have hit a nerve in these women with our questionnaire

24. Lederer also cites two other examples of foreign word parts oxymoronically drawn to each other pianoforte meaning soft-loud and sophomore meaning wise fool The author adds jokingly "If you know any sophomoric sophomores you know how apt that oxymoron is

25. One of the things the researchers learned from the survey was the following the history of the american family since the late 1940s the earliest generation included in the survey has been one of dramatic trade-offs

8. 5 Key to Exercises

1. When my Italian friend calls me, she often says *ciao* instead of "goodbye."

2. The guest list consisted of Dr. David Waring, Ms. Beverly Barton, J.S. Goodwin Jr., Marcus Welby, M.D., Mrs. Thomas Huntington, and Miss Marple.

3. He wrote an angry letter about his winter heating bill to Cygnet Oil and The Gastly Corporation.

4. The weekly comic newspaper in Paris, *Le Canard Enchaine,* carried a scathing satire of a local politician.

5. In France, April Fool's Day is referred to as *poisson d'avril.*

6. *Sundance* catalogue, mailed from Salt Lake City, Utah, advertises *Cocuchas* pottery urns made by hand in Mexico "with clay mixed by bare feet from volcanic ash, sand, and water" and fired in charcoal pits.

7. Thirteen people were injured when a bus collided with a truck in Las Vegas, according to the newsletter, *The Last Word,* published in January, 2002.

8. In his book, *The Writer's Way,* author Jack Rawlins says that the way a baby teaches itself to talk is an excellent way to learn language skills.

9. Adam Gopnick, in his book, *Paris to the Moon,* wrote that the men of the *Paris Propre* come down his street every night to collect garbage.

    If you missed italicizing Paris, that's okay. It was not clear in the sentence that it was supposed to be a part of the foreign term.

10. In *Woe is I: The Grammarphobe's Guide to Better English in Plain English,* Patricia T. O'Conner, in a section called "A Cure for the Whom-Sick," writes: "Now for the good news. In almost all cases you can use 'who' instead of 'whom' in conversation or in informal writing, like personal letters and casual memos."

11. In their new 4,000-square-foot house, they had a 20-foot-by-20-foot library and a 10-by-12-foot exercise room.

12. In their book, *Better Spelling in 30 Minutes a Day,* authors Crosby and Emery say as follows: "'Media' is a plural form of 'medium'; therefore, we must say 'the media are' never 'the media is.'"

13. The students listed as their favorite foods Swiss cheese, Italian bread, Boston baked beans, and English muffins.

14. Mr. Jerome L. Tarp, Jr. is currently working for Pioneer Corp., in Dallas, and his cousin, Martin Tarp, took a position with Ashland Food, Inc., in Boulder, Colorado.

15. The professor of our class has just come back from teaching at a *lycee* in France and will return there to direct a program in concentrated *Francais-Anglais* next spring.

16. The President traveled on his private plane, *Air Force One,* to Germany last week accompanied by his wife and his staff of six.

17. The City Council is dominated by the Democratic party, but the County Tax Commission has a majority of Republicans on its roster.

18. The books on the shelf in my history professor's office include *Churchill,* by Martin Gilbert; *The Chief: The Life of William Randolph Hearst,* by David Nasaw; *The Trust,* by Susan E. Tifft and Alex S. Jones; *American Caesar,* by William Manchester; *Winchell,* by Neal Gabler; and *The Power Broker,* by Robert A. Caro.

    If you are not familiar with some of these titles, sorting these names out may have been a bit confusing for you—which simply proves the point: punctuation is critical to clear reading.

19. While studying French together, Calvin paused and said to Hannah, "I love you *beaucoup,*" which surprised Hannah so much that she replied, "I love you *de plus belle.*"

20. In his book, *Crazy English,* Richard Lederer defines "oxymoron" as "a figure of speech in which two incongruous, contradictory terms are yoked together in a small space," for example, "good grief."

21. Lederer, who frequently comments on National Public Radio (NPR), goes on to say that the word "oxymoron" is itself oxymoronic, because it is formed from two Greek roots of opposite meanings—*oxys*, meaning "sharp and keen," and *moros*, meaning "foolish"—the same root that gives us the word "moron."

22. For their study, *Iron, Bronze, and Golden Women,* the researchers surveyed 1,045 women by sending them a three-page questionnaire and were surprised when 81.2% of the women returned the completed survey document.

23. One researcher exclaimed in disbelief, "This is *amazing!* Nobody gets such a high return on surveys." Her partner was equally startled. *"What? An 80% return?* We must have hit a nerve in these women with our questionnaire."

24. Lederer also cites two other examples of foreign word parts oxymoronically drawn to each other: *pianoforte*, meaning "soft-loud," and *sophomore*, meaning "wise fool." The author adds jokingly "If you know any sophomoric sophomores, you know how apt that oxymoron is."

25. One of the things the researchers learned from the survey was the following: The history of the American family since the late *1940*'s, the earliest generation included in the survey, has been one of dramatic trade-offs.

Parentheses and Brackets

: — ; / • , ? ! " " ' ( ) - ;

Omit needless words! Omit needless words!
Omit needless words!

—Will Strunk,
Co-author of *The Elements of Style*

9.1 Parentheses

Use parentheses around elements that are interrupting your sentence—elements that are not necessary, but add to the clarity, comment on, or illustrate something in the sentence. One way of looking at parenthetical elements is that they are whispered asides within the sentence.

Examples:
- He had given a good answer to the question (though he wasn't aware of it), so the teacher asked him to clarify his answer, hoping he would then understand it more thoroughly.
- The pond is quite large (a neighbor said it is twenty-eight acres), but it looks tiny on the map.

[167]

- She was working in the dean's office (I know, I saw her there on Tuesday), and she asked me to fill out a new application.

 Tip Never put a comma before a parenthetical comment, but put a comma after it if the words or phrases before the parenthesis call for it. Remember, the parenthetical remark interrupts the sentence, so the sentence itself should be punctuated as if the parentheses were not there.

In fact, in editing your own work, look at the sentence *without* the parenthetical comment and make sure it is punctuated properly. Then read the sentence *with* the parentheses.

Example:

I told him I would meet him at the station, and he said that was convenient for him.

Now, if you want to add a comment about which station, write: I told him I would meet him at the station (the one at the far end of town), and he said that was convenient for him.

Sometimes, in a research paper, you will want to enclose your citations in parentheses. Consult the handbook you are using for formal research documentation or ask your teacher. But the general way to do that is the following:

"Have a point and make it by means of the best word" (Barzun, 1985).

This indicates that you are quoting Jacques Barzun, whose book, *Simple and Direct, A Rhetoric for Writers*, was written in 1985. If you use this or any other quotation, you should cite it fully in your Bibliography at the end of your paper.

Tip) A parenthetical statement may seem to you a bit like surrounding unnecessary comments with commas, or setting them off with dashes. You're correct. You can be the judge: If your unnecessary statement interrupts the sentence only a little, use commas; if it interrupts a little more, use parentheses; if the interrupting element is used for drama, color, or hesitation, use dashes.

Example:

> I saw the accident, but only from my rear-view mirror, as I was driving along 25A (on my way to the bank). Loud noises—a screech and then a crash!—attracted my attention.

Notice that the complete thoughts here are: *I saw the accident as I was driving along 25A, and Loud noises attracted my attention.* The "but" phrase, placed in commas, interrupts only a little. The "on my way" phrase interrupts a little more, so it is placed in parentheses. The "screech" and "crash" phrase is more interruptive and dramatic, so it is set off by dashes.

9.2 Brackets

Okay. You know how to use parentheses. Now, what do you do with material *inside* parentheses that you still want to explain or comment on? If you're an awkward writer and don't know what else to do, you put that stuff in brackets.

Example:

> The investigation into the problem (the killing of several people in Idaho, which had an impact on the National Rifle Association [NRA], and set off the media) has turned up some questionable suspects.

Tip Brackets are intrusive. They clutter your prose. You would use brackets [NRA] only if NRA was pertinent to points you would be making later in the piece ,and it was the first mention in a piece in which you would repeat the acronym again and again—and if you could not find a less intrusive place in the piece to give the acronym.

Usually you give the acronym immediately after the full name—in this case, The National Rifle Association—the first time you use it in your paper.

As a matter of personal taste, I would not write a sentence like that. I would write the following:

> The investigation into the killing of several people in Idaho, which had an impact on the NRA—The National Rifle Association—and set off the media, has turned up some questionable suspects.

▶ **Use Brackets to insert material into quotations:**

> "The governor said that he [Dr. Rogers] was originally in charge of the scientific project that produced the toxic material."

Tip Again, do not use brackets unless it is absolutely necessary. A good way around this clumsy use of brackets is to rephrase the sentence. Use indirect quotations where you can, or begin your quotation in a place at which you don't have to explain in brackets.

Example:

> The governor said that Dr. Rogers "was originally in charge of the scientific project that produced the toxic material."

) **Another way to use brackets is in a quotation that has a misstatement or misspelling in it, but you feel constrained to quote it directly.**

Examples:

* "Hemmingway's [*sic*] *The Sun Also Rises* is an American masterpiece," wrote the critic, G. M. Kenny."

The bracketed *sic* indicates that this is *exactly* the way the person who is quoted wrote the word.

* The critic, Kenny, misspelled Hemingway's name, so the person who is quoting the critic points out the fact that he, himself, knows the name is misspelled. In using [*sic*], the person quoting also suggests that if a critic does not know how to spell Hemingway's name correctly, she has dubious qualifications as a critic of Hemingway's work.

This is a good trick to know when you wickedly want to point out someone else's mistake.

9.3 Exercises

Punctuate the sentences below. These are tough because a lot is going on in these sentences. Never fear. You have some choices here, and in the key I will explain some things that may puzzle you.

1. I told Cynthia you know the woman in our art class that there was an exhibit she would enjoy at the Museum of Modern Art

2. The book reviewer wrote "Virginia Wolf *sic* wrote an essay called A Room of One's Own that influenced millions of women"

3. The movie was horrible I mean just *horrible* and I hope you don't waste your money on it

4. Families find comfort in assigning roles to their members when someone tries to break out of that role it causes immense dislocation of the whole structure director Daniel Sullivan remarked of the 1939 play Morning's at Seven.

5. Goldman said in his book *In Pursuit of Prestige: Strategy and Competition in U.S. Higher Education* that reputation is a measure of the customers' view of the institution

6. In his column *The New York Times* Jan. 20, 2002 David Bouchier writes that working at home he is a writer has its drawbacks because it is so easy to find other things to do.

7. Fifty years ago Robert Maynard Hutchins and Mortimer J. Adler University of Chicago put together a collection of books called *The Great Books of the Western World* 52 volumes that they considered the best books in the tradition of Western literature

8. David Brooks in his article Why the U.S. Will Always be Rich quoted John Adams as saying Human nature, in no form of it, could ever bear prosperity.

9. Louis Menand reviewing the film The Lord of the Rings: The Fellowship of the Ring in The New York Review of Books writes that it is "an impressive piece of filmmaking" moreover he says "it is intensely faithful to the text, although unsurprisingly a great deal of the story is omitted"

10. In writing about one of our country's fabled institutions the Central Intelligence Agency CIA Thomas Powers says in The New York Review of Books that the CIA was established in 1947 as a direct consequence of the failure to foresee the Japanese attack on the American naval base at Pearl Harbor.

11. "The House passed a bill HR 3525 calling for new background checks on student visa applicants from countries that the State Department considers to be sponsors of terrorism The Chronicle of Higher Education Jan. 11 2002 and the legislation would also require colleges and federal offices to monitor the movements of all foreign students in the US"

12. In January 2002 The Chronicle of Higher Education CHE which is often called The Wall Street Journal of Higher Education reports that Harry Potter and the Sorcerer's Stone is Number 1 on the reading lists of college students John Adams a biography by David McCullough ranks Number 8

13. The investigation into the attack on the World Trade Center which killed between 3,000 and 5,000 people and prompted the Central Intelligence Agency CIA to do some self-searching still continued ten months after the tragic event

14. The book cited a study by a medical organization American Medical Association AMA that spoke of work it was doing about exercise and longevity

15. Groups who have declared themselves opposed to censorship in the U S over the years include Action for Children's Television ACT the National Coalition on Television Violence NCTV the American Medical Association AMA the National Parent-Teacher Association NPTA and the National Council of the Churches of Christ NCCC

16. The New World Dictionary of American Language defines double-think sometimes written doublethink as illogical or deliberately perverse thinking in terms that distort or reverse the truth to make it more acceptable the word was coined by George Orwell in *1984* written in 1949

17. Do you know what the word lurdan means the teacher asked Roy who was nodding off in his seat in class When Roy admitted that he did not the teacher told him it meant a lazy dull person She told him the word could be used as an adjective or a noun.

18. Kim was looking for a biblical reference that would discuss truth he found two in John 14 6 and 17 17 and one in Ephesians 4 14

19. I wrote my cousin Dear Carol You remember the man I introduced you to at Carla's wedding the tall one with very dark hair who told the story about his grandfather well his name is Patrick Harman and we are going to be married next July what do you think of that

20. I volunteered during the break for an organization I believe in Planned Parenthood Federation of America PPFA and they gave me some very interesting work doing research on the attitudes of women across the country

21. My friend Charlotte volunteered with another social organization The Equal Employment Opportunity Commission EEOC which gave her some work she enjoyed too

22. Chris reported on an article titled Your E Mail May Be Bugged in the magazine American Lawyer that said Microsofts and Netscapes e mail programs are simple to use but easy to exploit

23. One of the teams in our class gave an oral report a detailed behind the scenes account of one of our countrys most hotly contested presidential elections drawing on a book called Deadlock The Inside Story of Americas Closest Elections, written by the political staff of The Washington Post

24. Jonathan and his group reported on the book The Constitution and the New Deal by G Edward White Harvard University Press which Jonathan characterized as A challenge to conventional wisdom about the impact of the New Deal on twentieth century Supreme Court decisions

25. My friend and I went to see the stage play Wonder of the World starring Sarah Jessica Parker at the Manhattan Theatre Club others in the cast were Mary Louise Burke Kevin Chamberlin Kristine Nielsen Bill Raymond Amy Sedaris and Alan Tudyk with a script by David Lindsay-Abaire

9.4 Key to Exercises

1. I told Cynthia—you know, the woman in our art class—that there was an exhibit she would enjoy at the Museum of Modern Art.

   Dashes set off a parenthetical remark. You might choose to put it into parentheses rather than dashes.

2. The book reviewer wrote, "Virginia Wolf [*sic*] wrote an essay called 'A Room of One's Own' that influenced millions of women."

   The author's last name is Woolf—which calls for the Latin term, *sic*, indicating that the book reviewer misspelled the author's name. An essay is a short piece of literature; therefore it is placed in single quotation marks.

3. The movie was horrible—I mean, just *horrible*—and I hope you don't waste your money on it.

   Dashes and italics are used here to add emphasis.

4. "Families find comfort in assigning roles to their members; when someone tries to break out of that role it causes immense dislocation of the whole structure," said director Daniel Sullivan of the 1939 play, "Morning's at Seven."

   You might have made two sentences of the one in which I placed a semicolon. That would be correct, too.

5. Goldman said in his book, *In Pursuit of Prestige: Strategy and Competition in U.S. Higher Education*, that reputation is a measure of the customers' view of the institution.

   Notice here the comma before *that*. Remember that we usually don't place a comma before *that*? This is true when we are considering necessary and unnecessary elements in a sentence. The use of *that* usually introduces a *necessary element*, which is not set off in commas. However, here the word "book" and the name of that book is an *appositive*. Appositives *are* set off in commas. Recall that one rule may sometimes overrule another? This is an example. When this happens—two rules conflict—use the rule that produces the most clarity in your sentence.

6. In his column (*The New York Times, Jan. 20, 2002*), David Bouchier writes that working at home—he is a writer— has its drawbacks because it is so easy to find other things to do.

   Here the citation is in parentheses. I have put "he is a writer," a parenthetical remark, within dashes because I have already used parentheses in the sentence. If you put it in parentheses, you are correct as well.

7. Fifty years ago Robert Maynard Hutchins and Mortimer J. Adler (University of Chicago), put together a collection of books called *The Great Books of the Western World*—52 volumes that they considered the best books in the tradition of Western literature.

   After "Western World," you might have correctly placed a comma or a colon. I chose the dash to set the 52 books off a little to emphasize the number.

8. David Brooks in his article, "Why the U.S. Will Always be Rich," quotes John Adams as saying, "Human nature, in no form of it, could ever bear prosperity."

Notice that this is not a direct quotation within a quotation, so both quotations here are placed in double quotation marks.

9. Louis Menand, reviewing the film, "The Lord of the Rings: The Fellowship of the Ring" in *The New York Review of Books,* writes that it is "an impressive piece of filmmaking"; moreover, he says, "it is intensely faithful to the text, although unsurprisingly a great deal of the story is omitted."

Notice that "the film," and the name of the film and its location, serve as appositives and are therefore set off with commas.

10. In writing about one of our country's fabled institutions, the Central Intelligence Agency (CIA), Thomas Powers says in *The New York Review of Books* that the CIA was established in 1947 as a direct consequence of the failure to foresee the Japanese attack on the American naval base at Pearl Harbor.

No brackets are needed. This acronym is not within quotation marks or parentheses, so you can put it in parentheses. You could, in fact, leave (CIA) out, because the second reference is near enough to the official name that readers are not likely to become confused.

11. "The House passed a bill [HR 3525] calling for new background checks on student visa applicants from countries that the State Department considers to be sponsors of terrorism [*The Chronicle of Higher Education,* Jan. 11, 2002], and the legislation would also require colleges and federal offices to monitor the movements of all foreign student in the U.S."

Though this is an intrusive use of brackets, you may find this example helpful when you are quoting material directly.

12. In January 2002, *The Chronicle of Higher Education* (CHE), which is often called *"The Wall Street Journal* of higher education," reports that *Harry Potter and the Sorcerer's Stone* is Number 1 on the reading lists of college students; *John Adams*, a biography, by David McCullough ranks Number 8.

    Notice that the two newspapers and two books are in italics. If you divided this into two sentences and placed a period where I placed a semicolon, you would be correct, too.

13. The investigation into the attack on the World Trade Center, which killed between 3,000 and 5,000 people and prompted the Central Intelligence Agency (CIA) to do some self-searching, continued ten months after the tragic event.

    The acronym was not inside quotation marks or parentheses, so you set it off with parentheses rather than brackets.

14. The book cited a study by a medical organization, the American Medical Association (AMA), that spoke of work it was doing about exercise and longevity.

    Here "medical organization" and the organization's title and acronym are appositives. Therefore, they are set off in commas before the word *that*.

15. Groups who have declared themselves opposed to censorship in the U.S. over the years include Action for Children's Television (ACT), the National Coalition on Television Violence (NCTV), the American Medical Association (AMA), the National Parent-Teacher Association (NPTA), and the National Council of the Churches of Christ (NCCC).

Again, since these acronyms are not within a quotation or a parenthetical statement, you may put them in parentheses. You may also separate each of these with a semicolon if you wish, since the acronyms in parentheses serve as a kind of internal punctuation.

16. *The New World Dictionary of American Language* defines "double-think"—sometimes written "doublethink"—as "illogical or deliberately perverse thinking in terms that distort or reverse the truth to make it more acceptable"; the word was coined by George Orwell in *1984,* written in 1949.

Well, this one should make you think extra hard. Put the words used as terms in quotation marks. Then put the directly quoted definition in quotation marks. You know to italicize the dictionary's name. Now, what do we do with the last part of the group of words? You can do as I did and separate the sentences with a semicolon, or you could start a new sentence by using a period and a capital letter. In this case, *1984* is the name of a book, but it was written in 1949. Look at how much information we were able to cram into these few lines simply by using proper punctuation!

17. "Do you know what the word, 'lurdan,' means?" the teacher asked Roy, who was nodding off in his seat in class. When Roy admitted that he did not, the teacher told him it meant "a lazy, dull person." She told him the word could be used as an adjective or a noun.

Here's another complicated one. You place "lurdan" in single quotation marks, because it is inside a quotation. Then you place "a lazy, dull person" inside double quotation marks, because it is not inside a quotation.

18. Kim was looking for a biblical reference that would discuss truth; he found two in John 14:6 and 17:1, and one in Ephesians 4:14.

An easier one at last! Note that biblical is not italicized or capitalized. I separated the two sentences with a semicolon. You may have wished to divide this into two sentences using a period. Notice the use of colons to separate chapter and verse.

19. I wrote my cousin: "Dear Carol, You remember the man I introduced you to at Carla's wedding—the tall one with very dark hair, who told the story about his grandfather? Well, his name is Patrick Harman, and we are going to be married next July. What do you think of that?"

    In this example, there is a lot of information to convey. The writer does it by quoting her letter to her cousin, into which she inserts a description of a man, and the news that they are about to marry. Breaking this material into three sentences—two questions and one statement—is a good punctuation solution here.

20. I volunteered during the break for an organization I believe in, Planned Parenthood Federation of America (PPFA), and they gave me some very interesting work doing research on the attitudes of women across the country.

21. My friend, Charlotte, volunteered with another social organization, The Equal Employment Opportunity Commission (EEOC), which gave her some work she enjoyed, too.

    Set off the two appositives with commas: *friend, Charlotte,* and *social organization, The Equal Employment Opportunity Commission (EEOC).*

22. Chris reported on an article titled "Your E-Mail May Be Bugged" in a magazine, *American Lawyer,* that said Microsoft's and Netscape's e-mail programs are simple to use but easy to exploit.

Well, I see here we have a comma before *that* too. Do you see why? Again it is because we have an appositive: *American Lawyer* is a renaming of "a magazine." Remember that one rule sometimes overrules another? This is the case here.

23. One of the teams in our class gave an oral report—a detailed behind-the-scenes account of one of our country's most hotly contested presidential elections—drawing on a book called *Deadlock: The Inside Story of America's Closest Elections*, written by the political staff of *The Washington Post.*

    Within the dashes is explanatory information. "Behind-the-scenes" is a compound adjective before the noun "account."

24. Jonathan and his group reported on the book, *The Constitution and the New Deal,* by G. Edward White (Harvard University Press), which Jonathan characterized as "A challenge to conventional wisdom about the impact of the New Deal on twentieth century Supreme Court decisions."

    Remember to capitalize proper names, government institutions, and programs.

25. My friend and I went to see the stage play, "Wonder of the World," starring Sarah Jessica Parker, at the Manhattan Theatre Club; others in the cast were Mary Louise Burke, Kevin Chamberlin, Kristine Nielsen, Bill Raymond, Amy Sedaris, and Alan Tudyk, with a script by David Lindsay-Abaire.

    You may have made two sentences using a period where I have placed a semicolon. That is correct, too. And you may have italicized *Wonder of The World.* You would have been correct either way.

Slashes and Ellipses

It is an old observation that the best writers sometimes disregard the rules of rhetoric. When they do so, however, the reader will usually find in the sentence some compensating merit, attained at the cost of the violation. Unless he is certain of doing as well, he will probably do best to follow the rules.

—Will Strunk

10.1 Slashes

Slashes have two uses: They mark line divisions when quoting poetry in text, and they can be used to separate alternatives.

▶ **Use slashes to mark line divisions when you are quoting two or three lines of poetry within your text.**

Remember to space before the slash and after it.

Examples:

- The last stanza in Emily Bronte's "The Night-Wind" reads: "And when thy heart is laid at rest / Beneath the church-yard stone / I shall have time enough to mourn / And thou to be alone."

- In George Eliot's poem "Brother and Sister," she writes: "He was the elder and a little man / Of forty inches, bound to show no dread, / And I the girl that puppy-like now ran, / Now lagged behind my brother's larger tread."

 Tip Don't let the genders here confuse you. George Eliot is a woman. (Her real name was Mary Ann Evans, but she took George Eliot as a pen name.) Notice, also, that when you write about literature, it's a good practice to write in the present tense—"reads" rather than "read," and "writes," rather than "wrote." Though the authors may no longer be living, the literature is. So we generally speak of literature in the present. Note, too, that you do not use a slash at the end of the last line you quote.

❱ Use a slash to separate alternatives.

No spaces before or after the slash are used with alternatives.

Examples:

- My daughter, Wendy, and I enjoyed reading the article about our grandmother/mother in *The Houston Chronicle*.

Note that the article is about Wendy's grandmother and the speaker's mother. Be sure you keep the order correct; if Wendy comes first, then grandmother should come first before the slash.

- Toby had a part-time job as waiter/bartender.

Toby's job is both.

- Beatrice married her stepbrother, so her main man is her husband/stepbrother.

10.2 Ellipses

Ellipses (the word is plural) consist of three equally spaced dots to indicate that something has been left out of a passage you are quoting. (You never want to mislead the reader, so just as you place everything you quote in quotation marks, you must indicate when you have omitted some words from a passage you are quoting.) Some stylebooks (for example, the Modern Language Association's stylebook, or MLA, which is most often used in writing college research papers) insists that you place these three dots in brackets [...] so readers will know that the ellipses are not a part of the original quotation.

 (Tip) If you find ellipses already existing within the passage you want to quote, do not put the brackets around them. For example: If the passage you are quoting had already been edited somewhat and reads, "Over the river... to grandmother's house we go." Use it exactly as shown, without brackets.

A passage from Charlotte Bronte's *Jane Eyre,* originally reads thus: "For several subsequent days I saw little of Mr. Rochester. In the mornings he seemed much engaged with business, and in the afternoon gentlemen from Millcote or the neighbourhood called, and sometimes stayed to dine with him."

(The odd spelling of "neighbourhood" here is not an error; this is the British spelling of the word.)

If you wish to quote only part of it, here is an example:

> "[...] I saw little of Mr. Rochester. In the mornings
> he seemed much engaged with business, and in
> the afternoon gentlemen [...] called, and
> sometimes stayed to dine with him."

An original passage from Kate Chopin's *The Awakening*, reads this way: "Edna had attempted all summer to learn to swim. She had received instructions from both the men and women; in some instances from the children."

If you wish to edit it somewhat, here is an example:

> "Edna had attempted all summer to learn to swim.
> She had received instructions from both the men
> and women; [...]."

Notice that you use the precise punctuation of the original passage just before the ellipses (here a semicolon), and notice that the quotation mark goes outside the final bracket. Why is there a dot outside the bracket? Good question. Because here we are omitting the last part of a quoted sentence, so you must show your reader that you have left off the end of the sentence by placing a period there. The last dot functions as a period, not as part of the ellipses.

You can also use ellipses just before a source citation in a paper that requires citations. When you do that, this is the way to write it:

> In *Whatever Happened to Jacy Farrow?* the author,
> Ceil Cleveland, writes on page 114: "One morning
> the door bell rang, and I greeted at the door one of
> my neighbors, a man who lived down the street.
> He was dressed in suit and tie, ready for work—I in
> shorts and T-shirt, ready for work—[...]" (114).

The original reads: "One morning the door bell rang, and I greeted at the door one of my neighbors, a man who lived down the street. He was dressed in suit and tie, ready for work—I in shorts and T-shirt, ready for work—and he seemed to have nothing to say."

If you want to omit the last part of a sentence, as I have done here, use ellipses, close the quotation, add the page number in parentheses, then close the sentence with a period.

 Tip) If all these dots and brackets seem trivial, remember that your job as a writer is to communicate precisely with your reader. You must not throw your reader off by failing to tell her exactly what you are quoting and what you are leaving out. And if you forget exactly how to use these special punctuation marks between writing one paper and another, keep this little book handy when you are writing and refer to it.

10.3 Exercises

Add all necessary punctuation to the sentences that follow and, when so instructed, format them as you would in a paper you are writing for class. Some additional space for your answers is provided on page 205. You may want to write or type the longer passages on another sheet of paper for practice.

1. Insert the poetry into the text and punctuate the entire passage properly.

    In Out of the Cradle Endlessly Rocking Walt Whitman writes

    Low-hanging moon!

    What is that dusky spot in your brown yellow?

    O it is the shape, the shape of my mate!

    _____

    _____

    _____

    _____

    _____

2. Insert the poetry into the text and punctuate the entire sentence properly.

    T.S. Eliot, in his poem called "Journey of the Magi" speaks of what we now call the Three Wise Men.

    A cold coming we had of it,

    Just the worst time of the year

    For a journey, and such a long journey:

    _____

    _____

    _____

    _____

    _____

    _____

3. Write this as you would in a paper for class.

    In M.E. Slack's poem, "I Wasn't Ready to Go to Bed," written in the voice of a young child, the poet writes: "I wasn't near ready / to go to bed; / but I had to do / what the grown-ups said. / I know what I'll do, / curl up in a ball; / I won't make a sound: / won't breathe at all. / I'll shut my eyes tight; / and cover my head; / lie perfectly still, / and play like I'm dead."

4. Punctuate the following and set it up correctly.

   Janet considered herself a daughter student consumer poet Here is her poem: Dad brings home the bacon / Mother fries it / Brother wont eat it / I at least tries it / This is all crazy / This is all rotten / All of the role divisions / Should be forgotten.

---

5. Janet's mother considered herself a mother housewife cook housekeeper driver psychologist.

6. Janets father considered himself an accountant mathematician commuter father.

7. Use proper punctuation.

    Danny is an actor bus driver He cant give up his day job that supports his passion for acting.

8. Use proper punctuation.

    James is a father caretaker He stays home with the children while his wife works.

9. Poet Emily Dickinson wrote these lines. Incorporate them in your paper. (Emily had some eccentric punctuation and capitalization. Quote them exactly as she wrote them.)

    Because I could not stop for death,
    by Emily Dickenson

    "Because I could not stop for Death— / He kindly stopped for me— / The Carriage held but just Ourselves— / And Immortality.

_____

_____

_____

_____

_____

_____

_____

_____

_____

_____

10. Use the following in text, but drop the first four words. This is a quotation from *The Yellow Wallpaper*, by Charlotte Perkins Gilman.

    "That spoils my ghostliness, I am afraid, but I don't care—there is something strange about the house—I can feel it."

    _____

    _____

    _____

    _____

    _____

    _____

11. Use the following in text, but drop the last nine words. This passage is from *Work,* by Louisa May Alcott.

    "Presently she looked up and inspected the girl as if a new servant were not more than a new bonnet, a necessary article to be ordered home for examination."

    _____

    _____

    _____

    _____

    _____

    _____

12. Use the following in text, but drop the last four words.
    The selection is from *Hyde Park Gate*, by Virginia Woolf.

    "The tea table however was also fertilized by a
    ravishing stream of female beauty—the three Miss
    Lushingtons, the three Miss Stillmans, and the three
    Miss Montgomeries—all triplets, all ravishing, but of
    the nine the paragon for wit, grace, charm and
    distinction was undoubtedly the lovely Kitty
    Lushington—now Mrs. Leo Maxse."

13. Here is the last stanza from a poem called "Solitude" from the book, *The Best of ME,* by M.E. Slack. Set it up as you would in a paper for class.

"My solitude is not retreat / to be apart from others; / it is a still retreat from where / I daily rediscover how much at heart / I am a part of others / all the others."

14. Here is another full verse from the same book and the same author. The title is "A Limerick at Sixty-Five and Holding." Set it up as if you were quoting it in a paper.

> I really am very conservative,
> Think proper nutrition imperative.
> Organic is prime,
> But at this point in time
> I will settle for any preservative.

_____

_____

_____

_____

_____

_____

15. Here's a quotation from James Hoggard's novel *Trotter Ross*. Quote the passage as if you were including it in a class paper, but omit the phrase "wherever she was."

> "Silently he told her, wherever she was, that he loved her, then immediately felt estranged from her presence."

_____

_____

_____

_____

_____

_____

16. Here is another line from the same novel. Include the passage in your paper, but omit the last six words and give the citation, page 137.

"He penciled a series of numbers on a piece of paper torn from a sack that lined the wastebasket in the kitchen and stuck it under the phone."

_____

_____

_____

_____

_____

17. Again from the novel, Trotter Ross, quote the following passage, but omit the words up to and including "pool."

"When it was dark and he and the other free guards had picked up the paper cups from around the pool, Trotter put on his shirt, then gathered the stuffed plastic garbage bags which lined the trashcans and dumped them into the two fifty-gallon barrels behind the pump house."

_____

_____

_____

_____

_____

_____

18. Here is a passage from In Defense of Women: Susan
    Rowson (1762-1824), by Dorothy Weil, in which she
    quotes a critic, Mary Sumner Benson. Quote the
    following passage and omit "and most important one."
    Notice that the passage already contains two ellipses.
    How will you handle that?

    "Women […]save for some unconvincing fiction,
    were not idealized figures on pedestals, but more
    ordinary creatures whose moderate education gave
    them a taste for the milder forms of literature but did
    not lead them to deep reasoning or serious study.
    They formed a part, and a most important one, of the
    community in their relation to men's pleasures and in
    their specialized duties as mistresses of the families
    […]" (Benson, 222).

_____

_____

_____

_____

_____

_____

_____

_____

_____

_____

_____

19. This passage is from *The White Peacock,* page 177, by
    D.H. Lawrence. Set this up as if you were writing a paper
    for class.

    "Having reached that point in a woman's career
    when most, perhaps all, of the things in life seemed
    worthless and insipid, she had determined to put up
    with it, to ignore her own self, to empty her own
    potentialities into the vessel of another or other, and
    to live her life at second hand."

    _____

    _____

    _____

    _____

    _____

    _____

    _____

    _____

    _____

20. Here is another passage from *Whatever Happened to Jacy
    Farrow?* by Ceil Cleveland. Quote this as if you were
    using it in a school paper, but omit these two sentences:

    "Her apartment is tiny, but pretty and cozy with
    chintz flowers on sofa and chairs. Geraniums bloom
    in the window boxes, and English ivy hangs from
    ceiling planters."

The full passage reads:

"Hello. I'm speaking to you on September 12, 1976, from our new home in Liz's third-floor apartment on West 79th. Liz is away on a month's vacation to Greece. Her apartment is tiny, but pretty and cozy with chintz flowers on sofa and chairs. Geraniums bloom in the window boxes, and English ivy hangs from ceiling planters. The bed is big and puffy, but, alas, there is only one. Paul, my son, has to sleep on the sofa in the living room. Or sometimes we swap. The way it works is this: The one who gets the bed has to take the cats, Honey and Gravy, who love to crawl over your face while you try to sleep."

21. In this passage from *Truth and Consequences: How Colleges and Universities Meet Public Crises,* Jerrold K. Footlick writes of the trials of Woody Hayes, football coach of Ohio State University (OSU) for 28 years. Use the material as if you were incorporating it into the text of a school paper. Omit "March 17, 1987, and from a humanitarian perspective he may have been right."

Here is the full text:

"Those eight years 'were the greatest years of his life,' pronounced Richard Nixon, who flew to Columbus to eulogize Hayes at a memorial service March 17, 1987, and from a humanitarian perspective he may have been right. Eight hours after the Clemson eruption, Woody had been fired, and it was as if the steam had been released from a volcano."

_____

_____

_____

_____

_____

_____

_____

_____

_____

_____

_____

22. This passage is from the same book, but on another subject. Incorporate the passage below in your paper omitting "That position proved not to be firm enough, as."

"That position proved not to be firm enough, as Hackney recalled during our conversation in his spacious National Endowment for the Humanities (NEH) office at the elaborate Old Post Office Building: 'The day the papers were seized, it bubbled all through the day; there were people running, there were confrontations, there were mass meetings, there was a tremendous amount of pressure.'"

_____

_____

_____

_____

_____

_____

_____

_____

_____

_____

_____

_____

23. Finally, from the book above, use the following passage in your paper, but omit "who by necessity have become marketing experts," and "staffed with skilled, experienced, well-remunerated professionals."

"Universities have understood for years the importance of having strong development offices. They have learned more recently the value of good admissions officers, who by necessity have become marketing experts. Yet fewer institutions have grasped the importance of building a powerful public affairs office, staffed with skilled, experienced, well-remunerated professionals."

24. From Charles Dickens' *Bleak House*, in the chapter "Jarndyce and Jarndyce." Treat this quotation as if it were within your paper, but omit all the words after "once more."

   "Being of age now and having taken the step I have taken, I consider myself free from any accountability to John Jarndyce; but Ada being still a ward of the court, I don't yet ask her to renew our engagement. When she is free to act for herself, I shall be myself once more and we shall both be in a very different worldly circumstances, I believe."

25. This is from a memoir, *Whatever Happened to Jacy Farrow?* by Ceil Cleveland. Write the passage, punctuating it properly, as if you were inserting it into a paper, omitting the first two words and the phrase "though we did not know the dead person."

"One day, when I was about eight years old, school was dismissed for a funeral. My little sister, Lucy Jane, and I went with the other children to the church, though we did not know the dead person. I was determined to see the corpse and casket, so I found a spot up close to the grave and tiptoed around there, my eyes glued to the moving casket. Well, the empty spot I had scouted out was the open grave, and I wound up—or rather down—in the bottom of it, just as the pallbearers were about to unload their goods. I looked up and saw the bottom of the casket coming at me and squealed in terror. A shocked man pulled me out of the grave."

Answers:

_____

_____

_____

_____

_____

_____

_____

_____

_____

_____

_____

_____

_____

_____

_____

_____

_____

_____

_____

_____

_____

_____

10.4 Key to Exercises

1. In "Out of the Cradle Endlessly Rocking," Walt Whitman writes, "Low-hanging moon! / What is that dusky spot in your brown yellow? / O it is the shape, the shape of my mate!"

2. T.S. Eliot, in his poem called "Journey of the Magi," speaks of what we now call the Three Wise Men, "A cold coming we had of it, / Just the worst time of the year / For a journey, and such a long journey:"

3.
        I Wasn't Ready to Go to Bed
                M.E. Slack
            I wasn't near ready
            to go to bed;
            but I had to do
            what the grown-ups said.
            I know what I'll do,
            curl up in a ball;
            I won't make a sound;
            won't breathe at all.
            I'll shut my eyes tight;
            and cover my head;
            lie perfectly still,
            and play like I'm dead.

4. Janet considered herself a daughter/student/consumer/poet. Here is her poem:

            Dad brings home the bacon
            Mother fries it
            Brother won't eat it
            I at least tries it
            This is all crazy
            This is all rotten
            All of these role divisions
            Should be forgotten.

5. Janet's mother considered herself a mother/housewife/cook/housekeeper/driver/psychologist.

6. Janet's father considered himself an accountant/mathematician/commuter/father.

7. Danny is an actor/bus driver. He can't give up his day job that supports his passion for acting.

8. James is a father/caretaker. He stays home with the children while his wife works.

9. Because I could not stop for Death
Emily Dickenson

   Becaue I could not stop for death—
   He kindly stopped for me—
   The Carriage held but just Ourselves—
   And Immortality.

10. In *The Yellow Wallpaper,* Charlotte Perkins Gilman writes "[…] I am afraid, but I don't care—there is something strange about the house—I can feel it."

11. Louisa May Alcott writes in *Work,* "Presently she looked up and inspected the girl as if a new servant were not more than a new bonnet […]."

12. In *Hyde Park Gate,* Virginia Woolf writes, "The tea table however was also fertilized by a ravishing stream of female beauty—the three Miss Lushingtons, the three Miss Stillmans, and the three Miss Montgomeries—all triplets, all ravishing, but of the nine the paragon for wit, grace, charm and distinction was undoubtedly the lovely Kitty Lushing […]."

13. Solitude
M.E. Slack

    My solitude is not retreat
    to be apart from others;
    it is a still retreat from where
    I daily rediscover how much at heart

I am a part of others
all the others.

14. Here is another verse by M.E. Slack, titled "A Limerick at Sixty-Five and Holding."

> I really am very conservative,
> Think proper nutrition imperative.
> Organic is prime,
> But at this point in time
> I will settle for any preservative.

15. In *Trotter Ross,* James Hoggard writes, "Silently he told her […] that he loved her, then immediately felt estranged from her presence."

16. In James Hoggard's novel, *Trotter Ross,* he writes, "He penciled a series of numbers on a piece of paper torn from a sack that lined the wastebasket in the kitchen […]" (137).

17. Again, in *Trotter Ross,* the author writes "[…] Trotter put on his shirt, then gathered the stuffed plastic bags which lined the trashcans and dumped them into the two fifty-gallon barrels behind the pump house."

18. Author Dorothy Weil, quoting critic Mary Sumner Benson, in *In Defense of Women: Susanna Rowson (1762-1824),* writes; "Women…save for some unconvincing fiction, were not idealized figures on pedestals, but more ordinary creatures whose moderate education gave them a taste for the milder forms of literature but did not lead them to deep reasoning or serious study. They formed a part […] of the community in their relation to men's pleasures and in their specialized duties as mistresses of families…" (Benson, 222).

Notice that when you are quoting an author who has used ellipses, you omit the author's brackets. The three dots alone will tell the reader that words have been omitted. But you must add brackets to anything you omit from the passage when you quote it.

19. In this passage from *The White Peacock* by D.H. Lawrence, the author writes, "Having reached that point in a woman's career when most, perhaps all, of the things in life seemed worthless and insipid, she had determined to put up with it, to ignore her own self, to empty her own potentialities into the vessel of another or other, and to live her life at second hand" (177).

20. In a passage from *Whatever Happened to Jacy Farrow?* by Ceil Cleveland, the author says, "Hello. I'm speaking to you on September 12, 1976, from our new home in Liz's third-floor apartment on West 79th. Liz is away on a month's vacation to Greece [...] The bed is big and puffy, but, alas, there is only one. Paul, my son, has to sleep on the sofa in the living room. Or sometimes we swap. The way it works is this: The one who gets the bed has to take the cats, Honey and Gravy, who love to crawl over your face while you try to sleep."

21. In this passage from *Truth and Consequences: How Colleges and Universities Meet Public Crises,* Jerrold K. Footlick writes of the trials of Woody Hayes, football coach of Ohio State University (OSU) for twenty-eight years. The author writes "Those years 'were the greatest years of his life,' pronounced Richard Nixon, who flew to Columbus to eulogize Hayes at a memorial service [...]. Eight hours after the Clemson eruption, Woody had been fired, and it was as if the steam had been released from a volcano."

22. From the same book, but on another subject, Footlick writes "[...] Hackney recalled during our conversation in his spacious National Endowment for the Humanities [NEH] office at the elaborate Old Post Office Building: 'The day the papers were seized, it bubbled all through

the day; there were people running, there were confrontations, there were mass meetings, there was a tremendous amount of pressure."'"

Notice that when Footlick uses (NEH) he is not quoting anyone, so he puts the letters in parentheses. But when we are quoting Footlick, we should put the acronym in brackets.

23. Finally, Footlick writes, "Universities have understood for years the importance of having strong development offices. They have learned more recently the value of good admissions officers [...] Yet fewer institutions have grasped the importance of building a powerful public affairs office [...]."

24. In *Bleak House,* Charles Dickens writes in the chapter "Jarndyce and Jarndyce": "Being of age now and having taken the step I have taken, I consider myself free from any accountability to John Jarndyce; but Ada being still a ward of the court, I don't yet ask her to renew our engagement. When she is free to act for herself, I shall be myself once more [...]"

25. In *Whatever Happened to Jacy Farrow?* by Ceil Cleveland, the author writes: "[...] When I was about eight years old, school was dismissed for a funeral. My little sister, Lucy Jane, and I went with the other children to the church [....] I was determined to see the corpse and casket, so I found a spot up close to the grave and tiptoed around there, my eyes glued to the moving casket. Well, the empty spot I had scouted out was the open grave, and I wound up—or rather down—in the bottom of it, just as the pallbearers were about to unload their goods. I looked up and saw the bottom of the casket coming at me and squealed in terror. A shocked man pulled me out of the grave."

Postscript

Much more can be said about the way that those of us who speak English punctuate our sentences to ensure that readers can understand them easily. I have kept this little book, and the terminology it uses, as simple as possible. Of course, in that approach, some nuances of language are lost, for English is complex, and words have many connotations as well as denotations. As you feel more confident about punctuation, you can take some liberties that, for the sake of simplicity, I did not mention here. For your further reading, I have attached a list of books in the Bibliography. These books range from simple to quite complex in their descriptions of how language works. Pick up a few and try them. You may find something that this small book has not covered.

On the other hand, if you have made it this far through this book and have worked hard at correcting errors as you go along, learning new material on each page, you have every right to feel confident as a writer of clear, correct prose. You can punctuate your sentences as well as most people—and a good deal better than many. You should be able to chase down those "running boys" mentioned in the introduction—no matter how convoluted and complicated their paths become. If you have a particular question or comment, you are welcome to write me at *ceilc@optonline.net*. Please, write *Better Punctuation* in your subject line. Good luck—and remember how you get to Carnegie Hall.

All together now:

Practice,

practice,

practice.

Works Cited

Barzun, Jacques. *Simple & Direct*. New York: Harper & Row, 1985.

Beard, Jeffrey. "Your E-Mail May Be Bugged." *The American Lawyer*, May 2001.

Bouchier, David. "Working from Home, I Think." *The New York Times*, 20 Jan. 2002

Brooks, David. "Why the U.S. Will Always be Rich." *The NewYork Times Magazine*, July 2002

Chronicle of Higher Education. "What They're Reading on Campuses," 11 Jan. 2002.

Cleveland, Ceil. *Whatever Happened to Jacy Farrow?* Denton,Tex.: University of North Texas Press,1997.

Crosby, Harry H., and Robert W. Emery. *Better Spelling in 30 Minutes a Day*.Fraknlin Lakes, N.J.: Career Press, 1994.

Footlick, Jerrold K. *Truth and Consequences: How Colleges and Universities Meet Public Crises*.Phoenix, Ariz.: ACE Oryx Press, 1997.

Gopnick, Adam. *Paris to the Moon*. New York: Random House, 2000.

Hoggard, James. *Trotter Ross*. San Antonio, Tex.: Wings Press, 1999.

Iyer, Pico. "In Praise of the Humble Comma." *Time Magazine,* 1982.

Lederer, Richard. *Crazy English*. New York: Pocket Books, 1990.

Menand, Louis. "Goblin Market." *The New York Review of Books*, 17 Jan. 2002.

O'Conner, Patricia T., *Woe is I*, New York: Riverhead Books, 1996.

Powers, Thomas. "The Trouble with the CIA," *The New York Review of Books*, Jan. 17, 2002.

Rawlins, Jack, *The Writier's Way.* Boston: Houghton Mifflin, 2002.

Slack, M.E., *The Best of ME*. New York: Mill Pond Press, 1991.

Strunk, William Jr., and E.B. White. *The Elements of Style*. New York: Collier McMillan, 1979.

The NewYork Times Manual of Style and Usage. Lewis Jordan, ed., NewYork: Times Books, 1976.

Weil, Dorothy. *In Defense of Women: Susanna Rowson (1762-1824)*. University Park, P.A.: The Pennsylvania State University Press, 1976.

White, G. Edward. *The Constitution and the New Deal*. Boston: Harvard University Press, 2001.

Yeats, William Butler. *The Collected Poems*. New York: McMillan, 1966

Works Consulted

Allison, Alexander W., *et al*, *The Norton Anthology of Poetry.* New York: W.W. Norton & Co., 1975.

Baker, Sheridan. *The Practical Stylist. New York:* Thomas Y. Crowell Co., 1973.

Bernstein, Theodore M., *The Careful Writer: A Modern Guide to English Usage.* New York: Athencum, 1977.

Braddock, Richard. *A Little Casebook in the Rhetoric of Writing,* Englewood Cliffs, N.J.: Prentice-Hall, Inc., 1971.

Barzun, Jacques. *Simple & Direct.* New York: Harper & Row, 1985.

Belanoff, Pat, *et al,* *The Right Handbook.* Upper Montclair, N.J.: Boynton/Cook, 1986.

Bell, James K., And Adrian A. Cohn, *Handbook of Grammar, Style, and Usage.* Beverly hills, C.A.: Glencoe Press, 1972.

Brooks, Brian and James l. Pinson, *Working with Words,* Boston: St. Martin's, 1993.

Ciardi, John. *How Does a Poem Mean?* Boston: Houghton Mifflin, 1959.

Cleveland, Ceil. *In the World of Literature*, New York: Barron's 1991.

_____. *Iron, Bronze, and Golden Women*, Queens College of the City University of New York, 1994.

Crosby, Harry H. and Robert W. Emery. *Better Spelling in 30 Minutes a Day*. Franklin Lakes , N.J.: Career Press, 1994.

Editors, *The American Heritage Dictionary, Word Mysteries & Histories*. New York: Houghton Mifflin, 1986.

Flesch, Rudolf. *How to Write Plain English*. New York: Harper & Row, 1979.

Gilbert, Sandra M., and Susan Gubar. *The Norton Anthology of Literature by Women*. New York: W.W.Norton, 1985.

Goldstein, Norm, ed., *The Associated Press Stylebook and Libel Manual*. Reading, Mass.: Addison Wesley, 1994.

Gordon, Karen Elizabeth, *The Well-Tempered Sentence*. New Haven, C.T.: Ticknor & Fields, l983.

Hacker, Diana. *A Writer's Reference*. Boston: Bedford/St. Martin's, 1999.

Jordon, Lewis, ed., *The New York Times Manual of Style and Usage*, Times Books, 1976.

Lederer, Richard, and Michael Gilleland. *Literary Trivia*. Vintage Books, 1994.

O'Conner, Patricia T., *Woe is I*. New York: Riverhead Books, 1996.

Rawlins, Jack. *The Writer's Way*. New York: Houghton Mifflin, 2002.

Strunk, William Jr., and E.B. White. *The Elements of Style*. New York: Collier McMillan, 1979.

Index

`: — ; / • , ? ! " " ' ( ) - ;`

About the Author

Ceil Cleveland teaches writing and literature at New York University. A former vice president at the State University of New York at Stony Brook, and at Queens College of the City University of New York, she was for ten years editor-in-chief of *Columbia, the Magazine of Columbia University*. She is the author of four books, editor of seven, and has written more than one-hundred articles for national journals, magazines, and newspapers. She lives with her husband on Long Island.